The Dogs of Ireland

True Stories, Forgotten History, and Curious Trivia About Irish Dogs

Séamus Mullarkey

Copyright ©2025 Séamus Mullaevrkey

All rights reserved. No part of this publication may be reproduced, distributed, or transmitted in any form or by any means, including photocopying, recording, or other electronic or mechanical methods, without the prior written permission of the publisher, except in the case of brief quotations embodied in critical reviews and certain other non-commercial uses permitted by copyright law.

Plain Scribes Press

Paperback: 978-1-960227-67-6

Hardcover: 978-1-960227-66-9

DON'T MISS THIS SPECIAL BONUS

Do you want to learn more about Ireland?

This BONUS book has fascinating trivia, interesting tales and compelling stories about Ireland that you won't find elsewhere…

DOWNLOAD YOUR COPY FOR FREE

https://www.mullarkeysbooks.org/interestingireland

Table of Contents

INTRODUCTION 7
GUARDIANS BETWEEN WORLDS 8
THE DOGS OF IRISH LEGENDS 10
    Cú Chulainn - The Hound of Ulster..11
    The Cú Sídhe – Fairy Hound of Celtic Legend...........................11
    The White Hound of the Mountain 12
    Dobhar Chú, the Water Hound 12
    The Magical Hound of Lugh...13
    Fionn's Enchanted Hounds 14
    The Fiery Black Dog of Kilkenny 15
CONQUERORS AND THEIR CANINES 16
    Ancient Brehon Law: Dogs in Early Ireland 17
    Vikings and the Dogs of Battle...18
NORMAN LORDS AND MEDIEVAL IRISH DOG CULTURE 20
    English Influence and Evolving Dog Traditions.......................23
    19th Century: Early Welfare Reforms and Regulations 26
    Modern Irish Law: Welfare and Control in the 20th and 21st Centuries........28
IRISH DOGS IN POLITICS AND WARFARE....................................30
KERRY BLUES IN IRISH INDEPENDENCE.....................................32
DOGS IN ART 33
BLESSINGS AND CURES..36
IRISH SAINTS AND DOGS 38
DOG-RELATED SURNAMES...41
DOG PROVERBS 43
PLACE NAMES AND DOG LEGENDS..45
FRIENDSHIP WITH OTHER CREATURES.....................................47
    Ben the Labrador and Duggie the Dolphin...............................47
    George the Pyrenean Mountain Dog..48
IRISH BREEDS..49
    The Majestic Wolfhound...50
THE FAITHFUL TERRIERS..52
    Irish Terrier 52

Kerry Blue Terrier 54
  Soft-Coated Wheaten Terrier 56
  Glen of Imaal Terrier 57

SPORTING SETTERS AND SPANIELS 59
  Irish Red and White Setter 59
  Irish Red Setter 61
  Irish Water Spaniel 62
  The Enduring Kerry Beagle 63

DOG HEROES 65

UNDERDOGS WHO CAME OUT ON TOP 68
  Master McGrath: An Irish Racing Legend 68
  Kim the Jack Russell: A Roscommon Legal Drama 69

MODERN-DAY DOGGIES 71
  Breed Clubs 71
  Rescue Networks 72
  Advocacy and Social Media 73
  Therapy Programs 73

DOGGIE EVENTS 75
  Major Festivals 75
  Shows and Competitions 75
  Charity and Community Events 76

TEACH YOUR DOG IRISH 77

DOG-PRENEURS 79

IRISH DOG NAMES FROM MYTHOLOGY 81

IRISH-LANGUAGE DOG NAMES (AS GAEILGE - IN IRISH) 83

DOGS IN THE TOURIST INDUSTRY 85

A COUPLE OF LITERARY DOGS 87
  Maria, the Mischief-Making Spaniel 88
  Garryowen – Joyce's Mongrel Satire 88

SONGS 90

TV AND FILMS 93
  The President's Puppy Steals the Spotlight 94
  "Róise & Frank" – Canine Reincarnation 94
  "Man About Dog" – A Greyhound Caper 95

INSTAGRAM 96

THE SCIENCE OF "FINDING HOME"	98
IRISH DOGS - FACTS AND FIGURES	100
Legal Requirements for Dog Owners	101
TRAVEL TO IRELAND WITH YOUR DOG	102
THE FUTURE OF IRISH DOGS	104
CURRENCY, COMMERCE, AND CHINA	107
CONCLUSION	110
-ABOUT THE AUTHOR-	112
PLEASE LEAVE A REVIEW...	113
RECOMMENDED FURTHER READING	114
MORE FROM SEAMUS MULLARKEY	115
DON'T MISS THIS	121
SPECIAL BONUS	121
FOLLOW ME	122
DISCLAIMER	123

Introduction

In Irish life, dogs have been companions, guardians, hunters, helpers, links to the other world, and sometimes otherworldly themselves. We'll meet them all. The sleek hunters at a mighty lord's side and the shaggy bog dogs that warned of storms. The gentle giant at a president's side during TV broadcasts, and the lovable little terrier who attends Mass on a regular basis

The documentation of Ireland's dogs is often fragmented, contradictory, and incomplete. Breeders of famous strains are deceased, their families scattered, and their homes sold. Coveted illustrations have found their way to the rubbish heap, and many pedigrees of historic value may have been used for lighting fires. Still enough historical evidence remains for us to piece together an engaging (and I hope entertaining) overview of the key role dogs have played in Irish life down through the centuries. Prepare to meet the remarkable canines who have shaped Ireland's past and continue to enrich its present, demonstrating why, across centuries, the dog remains not just a pet or help, but a vital part of the Irish heart and soul.

Guardians between Worlds

The Irish imagination understood a dog's keen powers of perception long before modern science did. In Irish folklore, a dog's behavior could be a sign of things to come: a pacing, agitated dog predicted a visitor, a howling dog warned of death, and a dog who stayed away from a particular area was aware of a spirt presence it was best to avoid. In the past, a pregnant woman's dog was considered her guardian against evil fairies who might want to harm the unborn child or whisk the newborn away to their realm and leave a malevolent fairy child, or changeling, in its place. Under the Brehon laws, the old Gaelic legal code that didn't die out until the 17th century, if someone killed such a dog that was guarding a pregnant woman, they had to pay for a priest to pray over the woman nonstop until birth, to ward off otherworldly mischief.

Dogs also played a key role at the end of people's lives. They would howl as a sign of impending death. After a person's death dogs were supposed to see the deceased's spirit rising from the body and taking its leave, and their yelps or movements would be the same as if acknowledging a living human who was departing. On a more ominous note, people were afraid that ghostly hounds could snatch a soul as it departed its body and they would scatter bread, hoping it would distract the spirit-stealing canines and let the soul pass freely to the next world.

Dogs would also return to this earthly realm after their deaths for one last goodbye and there are numerous accounts of dogs' ghosts crossing their owners' paths and then vanishing, when the owners were returning home, only for the owner to hear the dog had died at home about the time the owner had seen them on the road.

The Dogs of Irish Legends

Dogs hold a significant place in Irish mythology, appearing in numerous legends and folktales. From loyal companions to ferocious guardians and even mystical creatures, canines often play pivotal roles in the ancient narratives of Ireland. The tales intertwine bravery, loyalty, and sometimes tragedy, showcasing the diverse ways dogs have been immortalized in Irish folklore.

Cú Chulainn - The Hound of Ulster

Cú Chulainn is a prominent hero in Irish folklore, renowned for his superhuman fighting abilities His stories are central to the Ulster Cycle, an ancient body of Irish myth. A famous statue of him stands in the General Post Office (GPO) in Dublin, site of the 1916 Easter Rising, commemorating his role in Irish national identity.

In Irish mythology, the boy Sétanta earned the name Cú Chulainn ("Hound of Culann") by slaying a blacksmith's ferocious guard dog when it lunged at him. One evening, arriving late to a feast at the smith Culann's house, young Sétanta, for this was the hero's name at birth, found the gate barred by a monstrous hound, famed for keeping thieves and warriors alike at bay. With only his hurley stick and ball, he defended himself, striking the hound with deadly accuracy. The guests rushed outside to see the boy standing over the fallen canine. Seeing Culann's grief at the death of his guard dog, Sétanta swore to protect the smith's forge himself until a new pup could be reared. From that night he was no longer just a boy—he was Cú Chulainn, the Hound of Culann.

The Cú Sídhe – Fairy Hound of Celtic Legend

In Celtic folklore, an eerie otherworldly hound called the Cú Sídhe ("fairy hound") prowls the land after nightfall. This terrifying apparition is said to be as large as a calf and sometimes green in color – a hue tied to fairy magic and misfortune. Tales describe the Cú Sídhe as a bringer of death whose unearthly baying could spirit an unwary soul away. In Irish folklore these phantom hounds haunt ancient raths (ringforts) and fairy mounds, guarding them. The name Cú Sídhe comes from the Irish Gaelic tongue: Cú meaning hound and Sídhe meaning fairy. Many a traveler on a lonely night road was on the lookout for a large shadow with glowing eyes, fearful the dreaded fairy hound might appear.

The White Hound of the Mountain

In 1903, in the rugged landscapes of County Mayo, Douglas Hyde, a folklorist, and future president of Ireland, recorded a captivating tale. Known in Irish as Cú Bán an tSléibhe, or "The White Hound of the Mountain," this story is a twist on the "animal-bridegroom" motif, a type of story found in cultures all over the world where a human marries a seemingly animalistic figure.

Our story begins with a curious prince, cursed to live a dual existence: a man by night, but a beautiful white hound by day. He lived in the remote hills of the western county of Mayo, his true form a secret to all. His life changed when he met a princess, who, against the wishes of her family, fell for the mysterious creature and agreed to marry him.

When the princess, pressured by her family, revealed the prince's dual existence, the prince vanished. He had been spirited away by a powerful witch's curse to a distant, enchanted realm. To save her love, the princess embarked on a perilous quest, facing trials and making magical bargains with mystical figures she met along the way. Her journey culminated in a confrontation with the witch, a final act of courage that broke the curse and reunited her with her prince.

Dobhar☐Chú, the Water Hound

In the shadowy depths of lakes in the West of Ireland, an ancient terror is said to lurk. This Hound of the Deep is a monstrous aquatic beast that can grow up to seven feet in length. It possesses the powerful, sinuous body of a giant otter, designed for rapid and silent movement through water, but with the head of a fearsome hound. The creature's lair is in the deepest parts of the lakes, where it waits silently.

While the stories of the Hound of the Deep might sound like pure fantasy, they are supported by some compelling local accounts. The most famous and detailed is a grim legend from the 17th century involving a local man named Conchobhar Mac Neill. According to the tale, the monstrous dobhar-chú emerged from Glenade Lough in County Leitrim and killed his wife, Gráinne. Enraged, Conchobhar hunted down and killed the beast. However, the creature's mate emerged from the water and relentlessly pursued him across the land in a terrifying act of revenge. This chase ended with the death of Conchobhar, and his tombstone in Conwal Cemetery is said to depict the monstrous creature and a sword, serving as a chilling reminder of the event.

The Magical Hound of Lugh

In the ancient tales of Ireland, dogs were more than just companions; they were beings of immense magical power. One of the most enchanting of these was the hound of the great god Lugh, a mythical creature with abilities that were both whimsical and potent. This magnificent dog was a legendary figure in 12th-century ballads and lore.

This hound's most astonishing ability was to transform fresh water into delicious mead, an alcoholic beverage made by fermenting honey. Such power made it a prized possession and a symbol of abundance and celebration. But this was not its only gift. As a companion to the heroic god Lugh of the Tuatha Dé Danann, the dog was also a formidable warrior. Its strength was said to be unmatched, its ferocity in battle a terrifying sight to its master's enemies.

Fionn's Enchanted Hounds

To understand the place of dogs in Irish legend, one must first get acquainted with Fionn MacCool. A legendary hunter-warrior and the leader of the Fianna, a band of legendary warrior hunters in ancient Ireland resembling in some ways King Arthur's Knights of the Round Table. Fionn and the Fianna's stories are so foundational to Irish culture that every schoolchild in the country knows Fionn name and his heroic deeds. Fionn's most beloved companions were his two hounds, Bran and Sceólan, dogs of extraordinary loyalty and uncanny insight.

The bond between Fionn and his hounds was unique because they were, in a very real sense, family. In a strange twist of magic, a sorcerer had turned Fionn's aunt, Uirne, into a dog. While in this enchanted form, she gave birth to two pups. Even after the spell was broken and Uirne returned to her human shape, her two offspring remained in their canine form. These pups, Bran and Sceólan, were adopted by Fionn and grew to be his constant and most trusted companions. This remarkable connection was put to the test in the story of Fionn's great love, Sadhbh. A druid, jealous of Fionn and Sadhbh's love, cast a spell on Sadhbh and turned her into a gentle deer, a form from which she could not return to human shape. Fionn, out on a hunt, was about to pursue the beautiful creature when Bran and Sceólan intervened. While the other hunting hounds saw only their prey, Bran and Sceólan recognized the deer as their human kin in animal form. They refused to chase her, instead running to her side and protecting her from the other dogs. Thanks to their intervention and loyalty, Sadhbh was saved from the hunt and eventually returned to human form, going on to become Fionn's wife.

The Fiery Black Dog of Kilkenny

In the twisting, medieval streets of the city of Kilkenny, legends tell of a canine spirit of an extremely sinister nature. This terrifying hound is often described as being as large as a donkey. Its powerful form was said to stalk silently through the city's cobblestone lanes at midnight, a sight that would surely terrify anyone who happened to see it.

This terrifying legend was still very much alive in the late 1930s, when students shared traditional tales from their parents and grandparents as part of the Irish Folklore Commission's Schools' Collection outreach program. In these accounts, the dog's eyes glowed like blazing coals, and twin streams of flame came from its mouth with every breath. The dog was said to haunt not only the city's darkest lanes but also its churchyards and graveyards. To encounter this hound was considered a terrible omen. The legends warned that anyone unlucky enough to lay eyes on the beast would "never have an easy mind again," their peace shattered by the chilling memory of the monstrous apparition.

Conquerors and Their Canines

Ireland's history was shaped by waves of settlers and invaders, each leaving an indelible mark on Irish culture. From the ancient Celts, who established a vibrant indigenous society, to the arrival of the Vikings, Normans, and later the English, each group introduced new customs, technologies, languages, and legal frameworks.

Dogs have been an integral part of Irish life for millennia, valued as hunters, guardians, and companions. Each wave of in invaders in Ireland – the Vikings, Normans, and English – interacted with and influenced Irish "dog culture" in unique ways. Long before the arrival of these invaders, however, Ireland's own native legal tradition had already enshrined the importance of dogs.

Ancient Brehon Law: Dogs in Early Ireland

Early Irish society, governed by the Brehon laws, placed significant value on dogs and wove them into its legal codes. The Brehon law (Ireland's indigenous legal system up to the 17th century) detailed everything from dog ownership rights to animal welfare. Dogs were classified and regulated according to their role and their owner's social status. For example, only the high nobility (kings and chieftains) was permitted to own the great Irish wolfhound, and the number of dogs one could keep was dictated by rank. These laws effectively made the wolfhound a symbol of status and restricted its ownership to the ruling class. Dogs of other types (such as herding or guard dogs) were likewise classified in a hierarchy of ownership and value.

Brehon law was remarkably detailed and even forward-thinking in animal welfare. It treated many animals almost like members of the community, giving them certain legal protections. Cruelty was explicitly forbidden – "It is illegal to override a horse, force a weakened ox to do excessive work, or threaten an animal with angry vehemence which breaks bones," warns one ancient tract. If an animal killed a person, however, the creature could be executed just as a human would be for such a killing.

Owners were held strictly liable for harm or mischief caused by their dogs, If a dog injured someone or damaged property, its owner had to pay a fine or ereic (compensation) according to the degree of the harm caused. A large section of one legal tract deals with dog fights – setting out fines for injuries caused to people trying to stop or encourage a fight. This suggests dog fighting was known in that society and had to be regulated. There were even provisions for accidents involving animals. For instance, if a person wandered uninvited into a place where a guard dog was loose and was bitten, the law weighed whether the person had been warned of the risk.

Some Brehon-era dog laws were rather colorful and specific, offering a vivid glimpse into daily life.

- Notices of females in heat: Owners of a female dog in heat were required to notify their neighbors in the four nearest townlands when the dog came into season. This provision was likely meant to prevent unwanted matings or canine scuffles – essentially an ancient "leash law" for breeding control.

- "Pooper scooper" law: If a dog committed a nuisance on a neighbor's land, the owner was obliged to remove the mess and compensate the neighbor with goods. One text specifies that the owner had to clean up the droppings and pay the neighbor with an amount of butter, curds, or dough equal in weight to the offending feces. In short, medieval Irish dog owners literally paid for not picking up after their pets! Every unpicked-up poop would cost you…

Vikings and the Dogs of Battle

When Scandinavia's Vikings began raiding and settling in Ireland (from the late 8th century onward), they quickly took note of Ireland's giant hounds. These massive Irish war dogs – forebears of today's Irish wolfhound – were so impressive that Vikings seized them as spoils of war and presented them as prestigious gifts to those they wanted to impress. All told, the Viking age in Ireland cemented the reputation of the Irish wolfhound as a near-mythic animal – a giant, fearless creature coveted from Dublin to Scandinavia. Archaeological finds in Dublin show that large "guard or battle-type" dogs were present in Viking settlements. Everyday life in Ireland's Viking towns also featured more ordinary dogs. By the Viking

Age (800–1000s), people did not have defined "breeds" as we know them, but there were distinct types of dogs serving different roles:

- Small lap dogs – kept by high-status women for companionship.

- Medium-sized dogs – vermin killers and herders that protected livestock from pests.

- Large hunting hounds – used to track and run down game in the forests.

- Powerful guard/war dogs – employed by both Vikings and Irish chiefs to defend homesteads and accompany warriors into combat.

Norman Lords and Medieval Irish Dog Culture

The arrival of the Normans in the 12th century (starting in 1169) ushered in a new chapter for Ireland's dogs. The Anglo-Norman knights and nobles who settled in Ireland brought continental hunting traditions and likely some of their own breeds, as well as also eagerly embracing the native Irish hounds.

One notable Norman contribution was the introduction of specialized scent hounds and structured hunt practices. On the continent the Normans had breeds like the St. Hubert Hound (ancestor of the bloodhound) and the now-extinct Norman Hound – a large, deep-voiced dog renowned for stamina if not speed. In Ireland, Norman nobles established enclosed deer parks and organized grand par-force hunts (chasing deer with hounds) similar to those in England and France. This was a departure from Gaelic hunting customs: early Irish law texts mention hounds, but the native method for hunting deer was often to trap them in pits or with snares, rather than long chases. The Normans helped popularize the thrill of the chase using dogs. For example, by the early 1500s the mighty Earl of Ossory kept an enormous hunting kennel: 24 mounted huntsmen with 60 greyhounds for stag-hunting, plus additional packs of hounds for hunting hares and even martens (small predators from the weasel family).

Despite their French pedigree, the Norman-Irish elite also cherished the native Irish wolfhound. These giant hounds continued to serve as status symbols and gifts for diplomatic purposes, such as ensuring goodwill or gaining favors, throughout the medieval period. Historical records show that English monarchs coveted them. King Henry VIII, for instance, maintained Irish wolfhounds and even issued a patent granting some as prestigious gifts to Spanish aristocracy. Within Ireland, Norman lords themselves adopted the Gaelic custom of exchanging fine hounds as tokens of alliance or goodwill. The 12th-century *Topographia Hibernica* by Gerald of Wales praises the Irish wolf-dog's courage and size, reflecting Norman admiration for these animals.

Life in Norman Ireland also saw dogs integrated into domestic and military spheres. Castles and manors had their guard dogs – it was common to see a big wolfhound or mastiff guarding the gate. In Waterford (a Viking-founded city later ruled by Normans), archaeologists discovered an iron dog collar from the 12th century, the oldest in Ireland. This ornate collar attests that even in Norman times, dogs were kept not just as working animals but as beloved companions (the collar likely adorned a favored hunting dog or pet). Ladies in Norman-Irish society sometimes kept small "comfort" dogs as well, echoing the Viking trend of lapdogs for well-bred rich women. A 14th-century account even notes that the Norman-Irish gentry would travel with their entire retinue of family, retainers, and hounds in tow, boarding with Gaelic chiefs during hunting forays – and it was expected that the hosts feed the dogs bread and milk as well as the people! This practice, known as coshering, shows how deeply interwoven dogs were in social rituals. Providing hospitality in Ireland extended to one's hounds!

Medieval folklore and literature of the Norman period also feature canines as central characters. One famous tale recorded by Norman chroniclers was the Werewolves of Ossory – a legend of an Irish family cursed to transform into wolves. In his chronicles, Gerald of Wales wrote of an incident where a priest traveling through Ossory, an ancient kingdom comprised of County Kilkenny and parts of County Laois, encountered two talking wolf-people.

In 1335, King Edward III sent a huntsman and two kennel boys to Ireland to collect 19 hounds from Irish lords. The mission's expenses, including the men's wages, the dogs' upkeep, and their sea passage, were all recorded in detail. This level of care reflects how highly valued these hounds were.

In fact, dogs owned by the nobility often enjoy a better life than many common people. The hounds of the Earl of Kildare, for example, were fed lavish amounts of bread and butter. Similarly, Lady Katherine Perm kept a staff of fourteen people just to care for her kennel, which was fed on bread and milk.

Medieval urban statutes also regulated dogs for public safety. In Norman-held towns of Ireland, curfew laws for dogs emerged. For example, a 14th-century rule required that dogs be kept leashed or enclosed, because roaming dogs caused "great injury and contentions." Any dog found wandering loose could be killed on sight by authorities – unless it was a nobleman's hound or a recognized hunting dog. This carve-out meant the esteemed breeds (greyhounds, spaniels, mastiffs used in hunts, etc.) were spared summary killing, whereas mongrels or "curs" owned by commoners had no such protection.

In Gaelic regions not firmly under Norman law, the Brehon traditions regarding dogs persisted for several centuries. In fact, the Brehon laws saw a resurgence in the 13th–16th centuries in many Irish lordships. However, the English Crown viewed the Irish legal system (with its "egalitarian" animal protections and status-based rules) as backward. The Statutes of Kilkenny 1367 – a set of laws intended to prevent Anglo-Normans in Ireland from adopting Irish customs – didn't explicitly mention dogs, but it exemplified the push to replace all Irish laws with English ones and would have covered all laws relating to animals.

English Influence and Evolving Dog Traditions

The English conquest from the 16th century onward introduced new breeds and customs that transformed Ireland's canine traditions. According to one popular theory, the origins of the Glen of Imaal Terrier can be traced to the late 1500s, when foreign mercenary soldiers hired by the English crown, settled in County Wicklow's Glen of Imaal, and brought their own dogs. These low-slung continental hounds likely interbred with local Irish terriers, leading to the development of a hardy, all-purpose farm dog. Some accounts maintain that these terriers were even used to power butter churns, a unique example of their role in daily Irish life.

The 16th–18th centuries saw England's grip on Ireland solidify, and with it came new laws that further changed the legal status of dogs. During the Tudor conquest in the 1500s, English authorities actively dismantled Gaelic institutions, including the Brehon legal system that had protected dogs. In 1603, the entire island came under the English Crown, and English common law became the only official law. This meant that those nuanced Brehon-era statutes about dogs were replaced by English legal concepts. In practice, Irish dog ownership now fell under the same rules applied in England: dogs were considered personal property, and the Crown and aristocracy asserted rights over hunting and game across Ireland.

The reputation of Ireland's native giant wolfhounds also continued to grow. These impressive animals were highly valued as tokens of high esteem and were eagerly sought after by monarchs from King Henry VIII to the King of Denmark. Their value was so high that in 1652, under Oliver Cromwell's government, an export ban was put in place to ensure enough wolfhounds remained in Ireland to help eradicate wolves. Cromwell's edict insisted that no Irish Wolf Dog be exported and that sufficient numbers be kept in Ireland to "reduce the wolf population," essentially recognizing these dogs as strategic assets of the state. At the same time, a scale of bounties was declared on wolves' heads – e.g. £6 for a female wolf, £5 for a male, and so on down to 10 shillings for a cub. Professional wolf-hunters, many using packs of wolfhounds, roamed the country under this policy. Thanks in part to these canine-assisted efforts, wolves were largely wiped out in Ireland by the late 18th century (the last wolf was killed in 1786).

Ironically, with their primary purpose gone, the breed nearly went extinct. The demand from abroad for Irish hounds was strong, and they were frequently given as diplomatic gifts. The Emperor Jehangir, the Papal Nuncio, the Spanish Ambassador, the Shah of Persia, and the kings of Sweden and Poland all received these hounds. Cardinal Richelieu, a powerful French statesman, even received a dog in exchange for a gold medal he had bestowed on Cardinal Ussher, an influential Irish archbishop.

At this time, the usefulness of dogs to humans also extended to the field of medicine. Even after death, a dog's value was not diminished. According to a 1729 Irish medical textbook, *Zoologia Medicinalis Hibernica*, various parts of a dog's body were used in folk remedies. For instance, its gall was mixed with honey to cure eye problems. An 18th-century work, An Essay towards a Natural History of the County of Dublin, notes that a dog's hair was spun into scarlet cloth, and its skin was made into leather for gloves and shoes, ensuring that every part was utilized.

The Penal Laws (late 17th–18th centuries) illustrate the link between human rights and animal ownership in Ireland. The Penal Laws were a series of harsh statutes imposed to subjugate Ireland's Catholic majority. While they primarily targeted land ownership, religion, and education, they also had indirect effects on who could own animals – including dogs. For instance, under a Penal Law from 1704, Catholics were forbidden to own a horse worth more than £. If a Catholic had a valuable horse, any Protestant could seize it upon offering £5 even if the horse's true value far exceeded that amount. This was intended to prevent Catholics from owning warhorses, but by extension it meant Catholics were barred from high-value property of many kinds. Although dogs are not explicitly enumerated in surviving Penal Laws, historians believe that similar class-based constraints applied to hunting dogs. A comment in a 17th-century context notes that "only the nobility were allowed to own sighthounds (greyhounds, wolfhounds, etc.)," implying any common Irish person found keeping such a dog might risk punishment.

Enforcement of these policies could be quite draconian. There are accounts of local magistrates ordering the confiscation or killing of "unlawful" dogs. To the English aristocracy in Ireland, a roaming Irishman with a greyhound was almost as provocative as one with a weapon. Meanwhile, the elites themselves avidly pursued hunting. The 18th century in Ireland saw the rise of formal fox hunting clubs among landlords, complete with packs of foxhounds and stag hounds. The game laws (many imported from English statutes) criminalized poaching – so if a landless Irishman used a dog to catch a hare or deer for food, he could end up in court or worse.

19th Century: Early Welfare Reforms and Regulations

The 19th century brought major changes to Ireland's legal landscape as Ireland was part of the United Kingdom during this time. This era saw the birth of animal welfare law and modern dog control measures, significantly altering legal attitudes toward dogs. Industrialization and urbanization created new problems – stray dogs, rabies scares, and public nuisances – prompting the government to regulate dog ownership in ways recognizable today.

One of the most important developments was the introduction of formal dog licensing. In 1865, the UK Parliament extended to Ireland a law requiring that all dog owners purchase an annual license for each dog. The first licenses were issued in 1866, costing two shillings per dog (a not-insignificant sum then) and recorded in detailed registers. This was essentially a tax on dogs, but it also had a public-order motive: to discourage irresponsible ownership and help identify owners of dogs that caused trouble. The dog license system endured – Ireland maintained it long after, well into the 20th century, and in fact, a form of dog licensing still exists today. Those historical dog licence registers have even become a resource for genealogists, indicating just how widespread dog ownership was despite the fee.

Under 19th century animal cruelty laws, a more favorable era for dogs in Ireland began. Irish humanitarian Richard Martin helped pass the Cruel Treatment of Cattle Act of 1822, the world's first law against animal cruelty. Later, the Cruelty to Animals Act of 1835 made it illegal to mistreat domestic animals and explicitly banned dog fighting, a major departure from Ireland's ancient Brehon laws which only fined people if someone was injured. These laws were enforced, and records show people were prosecuted for staging dog fights.

Concerns over public safety and disease led to new dog regulations in the 19th century. Rabies outbreaks in cities like Dublin prompted authorities to impose muzzling or quarantine rules. To protect livestock, trespass laws were updated to legally protect farmers who killed stray dogs attacking their animals, codifying a long-standing practice. This shows that while attitudes toward pets were growing more sympathetic, the law remained pragmatic about dangerous dogs.

The Dogs Act of 1871 introduced a proactive approach to dog control. The law allowed magistrates to legally declare a dog as dangerous and order it to be muzzled or destroyed. This was a significant shift, enabling authorities to take action to protect the public before another incident occurred, laying the groundwork for modern dangerous dog regulations.

By the turn of the 20th century, just before Irish independence, the legal framework for dogs was well-established. It included annual licensing, owner liability for damage, and anti-cruelty laws, with the Prevention of Cruelty to Animals (Ireland) Act 1911 consolidating the previous statutes. The law no longer reserved dogs for gentry, keeping them as pets was common across all social classes. Despite this change, dogs were still legally treated as a form of regulated property, much like a firearm or a cart.

Modern Irish Law: Welfare and Control in the 20th and 21st Centuries

After the foundation of the Irish Free State in 1922, dog laws evolved to focus on animal welfare, public safety, and responsible ownership. While initially retaining British legislation, Ireland gradually modernized its statutes to address new issues like specific breed regulations.

The Control of Dogs Act 1986 is the cornerstone of modern Irish law. It requires annual licensing and empowers local dog wardens to enforce regulations, seize stray dogs, and issue fines. The Act also mandates collars and ID tags, and in 2015, microchipping all dogs became compulsory, further helping to enforce licensing and reunite lost pets with their owners.

Modern law maintains the principle of strict liability for dog owners, a concept that dates to Brehon times. The Control of Dogs Act 1986 makes owners responsible for any injury or damage caused by their dog, regardless of prior behavior. This "no free bite" rule applies to both people and livestock and holds owners accountable when they are negligent.

The 1986 Act also addresses dangerous dogs. If a dog is deemed out of control, a complaint can be made to the District Court. The court may then order the owner to muzzle or restrain the dog, or in extreme cases, order its destruction. This process provides due process for owners while allowing courts to take proactive measures to protect the public.

A debated aspect of modern law is breed-specific legislation (BSL). The Control of Dogs Regulations 1998 list 11 breeds as "restricted," including the American Pit Bull Terrier and the Rottweiler. Owners of these dogs must keep them on a strong lead and muzzled in public, and they must be handled by a person over 16. Unlike the UK's 1991 Act, Ireland chose to restrict rather than ban these breeds.

Ireland has continually updated its laws to improve animal welfare. The Animal Health and Welfare Act 2013 criminalized cruelty and neglect, while the Dog Breeding Establishments Act 2010 introduced regulations to crack down on puppy farms. These laws reflect a shift from viewing dogs merely as property to recognizing them as sentient beings whose well-being is a matter of public interest.

The role of dogs in Irish society has led to some unique legal classifications. For instance, greyhounds are often treated as a regulated industry under the Department of Agriculture, with their own governing legislation like the Greyhound Industry Acts. This is a departure from general pet laws and shows how a dog's "job"—in this case, racing—can influence its legal status, echoing ancient ideas about a dog's role in society.

Irish Dogs in Politics and Warfare

According to a story in the Irish Examiner, a small Irish terrier-collie mix named Prince became an unlikely hero during World War I. His owner, Private James Brown from County Cork, was shipped out to the Western Front in 1914, leaving Prince behind with family in London. Terribly missing his master, the scrappy dog ran away and began an astonishing solo journey, eventually appearing months later in the trenches of Armentières, France. No one is sure how Prince managed the incredible feat, but he somehow found James's unit amid the chaos of war.

When Private Brown's comrades saw the mud-caked dog trotting through No Man's Land toward their lines, they couldn't believe it. But Prince leapt into his owner's arms, and the two were "reunited in a frenzy of delight" right on the front lines. The commanding officer was so impressed that he made Prince the regimental mascot. The troops fashioned a mini coat for Prince from an old uniform and gave him his own official ID disc. Prince not only lifted morale but also served a practical purpose in the miserable conditions by reportedly killing 137 rats in a single day, earning the gratitude of the entire company.

Prince survived the war, enduring close calls and even gas attacks while remaining by James's side. In 1918, he returned home to Cork with his owner. When asked how Prince found him in France, James would simply tap his chest and say, "Love guided him."

Kerry Blues in Irish independence

During Ireland's fight for independence, the Kerry Blue Terrier emerged as a patriotic symbol. The breed was so closely associated with Irish revolutionaries that they called it the "Irish Blue Terrier." The leader of the War of Independence, Michael Collins, was a devoted fan of the breed. He famously risked capture to clandestinely enter his purebred terrier in a 1920 dog show.

According to a report from the Irish Independent, the event was remarkable because it brought together British officers and Irish rebels who set aside their political differences for their shared passion for dogs. Collins's dog, cheekily named "Convict 224" to mock British imprisonment of Irish revolutionaries, won Best in Show. Other competing dogs had names like "Dawn of Freedom" and "Markievicz," after a rebel Countess. The breed became so iconic that Collins intended to make the Kerry Blue the official national dog of Ireland, but his untimely death prevented him from realizing this plan.

Dogs in Art

The revolutionary Countess Markievicz and her dog, Poppy

As well as featuring in history and folklore, Irish dogs have long held a special place in the country's artistic heritage. In the margins of the Book of Kells, the richly illustrated medieval Irish manuscript of the Four Gospels, a playful dog-like figure curls among the text, representing loyalty and companionship. This artistic canine tradition extends to ancient Celtic artifacts, and stylized dogs are often found on circular cloak pins and carved onto High Crosses—monumental public crosses with intricate designs. These carvings symbolize traits like hunting prowess and guardianship.

Paintings

Irish artists have long featured dogs in their work, often to represent loyalty and companionship. One notable example is Frederic W. Burton's 1841 watercolor, "The Aran Fisherman's Drowned Child." In this powerful image, a shaggy Soft-Coated Wheaten Terrier stands watch over a family's tragic wake, its presence highlighting the dog's role as a humble and devoted family friend. A century later, painter Jack B. Yeats used a canine companion to express a different emotion in his 1943 work, "The Man in the Moon Has Patience." The painting shows a lone traveler walking along a moonlit coast with a small dog by his side. The dog provides a sense of company, turning a solitary journey into a shared one.

Sculptures

Dogs are also a common sight in Irish sculpture, spanning from medieval times to the modern era. The tomb effigy of Robert Hartpole from 1594, located in Carlow, features a touching detail at the knight's feet: a small, stone dog curled up as an eternal symbol of fidelity. Time has damaged both the knight and the hound, but symbolism remains intact. The legacy of the Irish Wolfhound endures in several monuments. For example, a bronze statue of an Irish Wolfhound lies at the base of the Celtic cross memorial at Gettysburg, honoring the Irish soldiers who fought in the American Civil War. A similar wolfhound figure can be found on the monument to Daniel O'Connell, the "Liberator" of Catholic Ireland, in Dublin.

Another poignant depiction is Rowan Gillespie's Famine Memorial in Dublin, created in 1997. It includes a gaunt, starving dog following the emaciated human figures, embodying the desperate reality and suffering of Great Hunger.

Other contemporary sculptures celebrate canine loyalty in grand fashion. In 1998, a bronze statue of revolutionary Countess Markievicz was unveiled in Dublin, showing her in a casual stroll with her beloved cocker spaniel, Poppet. The statue offers a charming look at her life before the revolution. A much larger work is Lynn Kirkham's 2010 sculpture in Newbridge, County Kildare, depicting the legendary hero Fionn Mac Cool with his two enormous hounds, Bran and Sceólan. Standing on a roundabout, these steel figures symbolize protection and strength, bringing ancient Irish legends into the modern world.

Blessings and Cures

In traditional Irish folk belief, there were specific customs for how people interacted with dogs. One well-known superstition held that you should never say, "God bless the dog." Blessings were considered sacred and were reserved for people and holy objects. Giving a blessing to an animal, even out of affection, was thought to be a misuse of a holy gift and could even invite trouble from the fairy folk. So, instead of blessings, people showed their affection for dogs in more earthly ways, like with food or a kind touch.

Irish folk medicine also had a peculiar remedy known as the "hair of the dog that bit you." This was not just alluding to a hangover cure; it was an actual treatment. It was believed that if a person or an animal was bitten by a dog, a few hairs from the same dog could be applied to the wound to prevent illness. This was based on the ancient principle that "like cures like."

Old Irish Remedies for Rabies

Throughout history, people in Ireland used a variety of folk cures for rabies. Remedies included mystical items and concoctions. It was believed that the touch of the hand of a seventh son could heal a dog bite. Other cures involved applying a blessed cloven stick to the tail of the dog who bit you or washing a wound with specially prepared water. Recipes for these cures were passed down through generations. One such recipe instructed boiling herbs, garlic, treacle, and pewter filings in ale to create a medicinal drink.

Irish Saints and Dogs

Irish saints are often depicted with a deep respect for the natural world, including animals. Here are a few stories about Irish saints and their interactions with dogs.

St. Columcille:

Some traditions attribute healing powers to St. Columcille, a revered Irish abbot and missionary who helped spread Christianity in Scotland. He was said to have a special blessing for those suffering from a mad dog's bite, which included the prayer: *"Arise, through Christ be thou healed, in marrow and bone, and may the poison die in thee as I make the Sign of the Cross."*

St. Patrick:

The life of St. Patrick is closely tied to dogs. As a young man, he was kidnapped and enslaved in Ireland, where he worked as a shepherd. His only companions were the flocks and the sheepdogs that helped him with his duties. One legend says that his favorite sheepdog appeared to him in a dream, disguised as an angel, and instructed him to escape. The dog then led him to a ship that would take him home. The ship's crew, impressed by Patrick's ability to calm their restless Irish Wolfhounds, allowed him to board. Later, on his missionary journey, Patrick encountered the pagan prince Dichu. When Dichu commanded his massive war dog, Luath, to attack Patrick, the saint simply prayed. The dog, bewildered by Patrick's peaceful demeanor, stopped his charge and instead showed him affection, a "miracle" that led to Dichu's conversion and the founding of Patrick's first church.

According to a legend from the region of Ossory, a dog was the cause for a cathedral to be built in Waterford instead of a site in the townland of Connawee. The story goes that St. Patrick was planning to build a church there and had already laid the foundations. While he and his laborers were resting, a pagan woman offered him a bowl of broth. As a gesture of thanks, the saint began to eat but was horrified to discover a dog's paw in the bowl.

Kneeling on a stone, Patrick held his hands in a cross over the bowl and prayed to the Lord to restore the animal to life. Instantly, a yellow hound leaped from the dish and fled toward Waterford. Knowing the hound was now a creature of ill-omen, the saint commanded his workmen to chase and kill the beast to prevent it from causing widespread destruction. They caught and killed the hound a mile away and buried it under a whitethorn bush, which is still known today as Sgeithin-na-chon, or "The Little Thornbush of the Hound." The event was so unsettling that Patrick chose to abandon the building site, and the cathedral was later built in Waterford instead.

St. Colman:

St. Colmán, an Irish missionary to Scotland, was rarely alone, for his faithful dog was a constant companion on his journey. One evening, the saint and his dog sought shelter in the hollow of an oak. As Colmán rested, the dog took up a post at the entrance. The forest sounds gave way to a chilling silence, broken only by a low growl from the dog. Eyes, glinting with a predatory light, appeared in the darkness. A pack of wild wolves had found the saint and his canine companion. The dog, without a moment of hesitation, moved to block the entrance. It stood its ground against the snarling pack, allowing Colmán to remain safe inside. The standoff was a testament to the dog's tireless devotion; a bond forged in the wilderness that proved to be unbreakable.

St. Molua:

Another story involves Saint Molua, who founded a monastery in County Laois. His dog was known to sit faithfully outside his cell door during the day. In a testament to Molua's saintly influence, the dog would reportedly go to a nearby cave at night to lie down peacefully with a wild boar, turning two natural enemies into companions.

Dog-Related Surnames

Several clans proudly incorporated canine allusions into their family names, coats or arms, and battle cries. The O'Connors of Connacht, for instance, were a family of "hound lovers," a fact proudly embedded in their name, Ó Conchobhair. As famed hunters, their family's might was measured not just in lands, but in the packs of wolfhounds they kept at their heels. The last High King, Roderick O'Connor, used these noble animals to impress an English king in the 12th century. The O'Farrells of Longford were known for their fierce reputation, and their battle cry, "the rampaging dog," perfectly suited their name, Ó Fearghail, which means "man of valor." The MacNamaras, whose name means "son of the hound of the sea," alludes to an exceptionally brave hound that could brave both land and ocean.

The MacNamees, hereditary poets to the O'Neills, were aptly named "sons of the hound of Meath," using their words with the same spirited fervor a hound brings to the hunt. The O'Maddens were known as the "dog clan," their name rooted in the word for dog. Meanwhile, the Collins clan, with a name meaning "whelp," or young dog, demonstrated a scrappiness that helped them survive against larger foes. The Connellys' name means "fierce as a hound," and they lived up to it, with many becoming soldiers and leaders. The Conroys were "descendants of the hound keeper," a name of high honor that spoke to their ancestors' esteemed role in managing a king's kennels.

Even smaller clans had their own hound heroes: the O'Leavys had a famous chief named Cú Sleibhe (Hound of the Mountain); the Gilkennys a leader called Cú Geal (the White Hound); the MacGeoghegans a chief named Cu Calma (the Brave Hound); and the O'Mealas a leader named Cu Meala (the Honey Hound). In Connacht, the Maguires often used the name Chuchonnact (the Hound of Connacht), showing the widespread use of canine titles as marks of distinction.

The Talbots of Malahide in County Dublin, an Anglo-Irish family, had a direct connection to hounds in their very name. The word "Talbot" refers to an ancient breed of hunting dog, and their coat of arms proudly features a talbot hound. Their motto, "Forte et Fidele" ("Strong and Faithful"), sounds like a tribute to their emblematic hound, which stood as a constant reminder of their family's enduring loyalty and strength.

Dog Proverbs

Irish culture is rich with proverbs that use dogs to offer advice on life and human nature. One saying, "Is teann gach madra ar a thairseach féin." (Every dog is bold on its own doorstep), humorously notes that even the timidest dog becomes a fearless guardian in a familiar place. It's a reminder that we are all most confident and courageous in our own homes.

Another proverb, "Má bhuaileann tú mo mhadra, buailfidh tú mé féin." (If you hit my dog, you hit me too), powerfully demonstrates the depth of loyalty in Irish tradition. This phrase means that an attack on a person's dog is taken as a personal insult, reflecting a bond so strong that the two are inseparable. This sentiment is so old it's even echoed in the story of the hero Cú Chulainn, who offered to become a chieftain's new hound after accidentally slaying his dog.

Other proverbs offer practical advice. "Coinnigh an cnámh agus leanfaidh an madra thú." (Keep hold of the bone and the dog will follow you) is a clever saying about motivation. It suggests that if you have what someone wants, they will remain loyal to you—a piece of ancient wisdom about how to earn trust and companionship.

Finally, the saying "The old dog for the long road and the pup for the boreen" is a piece of practical wisdom. It suggests that for a difficult or long journey, it's best to rely on age and experience. The term "boreen" (from the Irish bóithrín, meaning "little road") firmly roots this saying in the Irish countryside, where a steady hand is more valuable than youthful exuberance when following a challenging path.

Place Names and Dog Legends

The Irish landscape is filled with place names that honor dogs, a testament to their cultural significance. The words "madra" and "mada," both meaning "dog," are often found in local names like Glenamaddy (Valley of the Dogs) in County Galway, which is said to be named for the packs of wolfhounds that once roamed the area.

Some places get their names from legendary canine feats. Limavaddy (Leap of the Dog) in County Derry is named after a heroic hound that, according to local lore, leapt across the River Roe to carry a message to its master, saving the clan's castle from siege. The ruins of a castle still stand there today, overlooking the river. Dogstown in County Meath, which in Irish is Baile na Madadh (Town of the Dogs), likely takes its name from kennels once kept by local nobility. Local folklore and anecdotes suggest the town was home to many dogs, who were both loyal companions and fierce protectors.

Lough Conn in County Mayo, whose name means "Lake of the Hound," is believed to be the final resting place of a beloved hound of the mythical warrior Fionn Mac Cumhaill, who drowned while chasing a magical boar. The mountain Slievawaddra (Mountain of the Dog) in County Kerry may have been named for a legendary guardian hound that lived on its slopes. Meanwhile, Lios na gCon (Fort of the Hounds) in County Cork is a medieval ringfort whose name suggests it was a stronghold where ancient chieftains kept and protected their prized hounds.

In the Slieve Mish mountains of Kerry, the ancient fort of Caherconree (Fort of the Hound King) is named after the legendary sorcerer-king Cú Roí mac Dáire, a figure from Irish mythology whose name translates to "Hound of the Battlefield." This dramatic fort was the setting for a showdown with another famous hero with a canine name, Cú Chulainn.

In the Irish landscape, even ancient burial sites honor the bond between humans and their canine companions. The Leaba na Con (Grave of the Dog) in County Kilkenny is a dolmen, or megalithic tomb, that folklore claims marks the burial place of a favorite hound. Similarly, a mound in County Galway is called the "Greyhound's Grave," suggesting that the Irish mourned their beloved dogs and honored their loyalty with lasting monuments.

Friendship with Other Creatures

Ben the Labrador and Duggie the Dolphin

One of Ireland's most heartwarming modern tales is the unique bond between Ben, a Labrador retriever, and Duggie, a wild dolphin. Around 2016, on Tory Island off the coast of Donegal, a lone dolphin named Duggie began visiting the local harbor after losing her mate. During his daily swim, Ben the dog met the dolphin, and the two quickly formed an extraordinary friendship. They were often seen swimming together for hours in the cold Atlantic waves, chasing each other and diving in perfect sync. Although Duggie would occasionally join other dolphin pods, she always returned to the shore to be with her canine best friend. Their remarkable interspecies bond captured global attention in viral videos.

George the Pyrenean Mountain Dog

At Comeragh Mountain Poultry in County Waterford, a large Pyrenean Mountain Dog named George serves as a livestock guardian, protecting free-range hens from predators like foxes and mink. The farm's owner, Clotilde Kiely, uses these dogs to allow her poultry to roam freely while remaining safe. As part of a "polycultural" and sustainable approach to farming, George's effectiveness is evident in the fact that the hens famously follow him around like a small "hentourage." When he was a young dog, he sometimes wore a muzzle to control his boisterous play, but his presence was enough to deter predators. George's story, which was profiled in the Irish media, helped raise awareness about the use of guardian breeds for poultry farmers throughout Ireland.

Irish Breeds

There are nine native breeds of dog in Ireland, but the majority of dogs on the island today don't belong to these breeds. This has led the Irish Kennel Club to lobby for heritage status to ensure their survival.

The nine native breeds are:

- **Terriers:** The Irish Terrier, Irish Soft-Coated Wheaten Terrier, Kerry Blue Terrier, and Glen of Imaal Terrier.

- **Gun Dogs:** The Irish Red and White Setter, Irish Red Setter, and Irish Water Spaniel.

- **Hounds:** The Kerry Beagle and the Irish Wolfhound.

Sadly, six of these nine breeds are now considered vulnerable to extinction. The ancestry of these dogs is difficult to trace, with most pedigrees only going back about 200 years. Even within that timeframe, many have changed significantly in appearance and temperament due to selective breeding.

The Majestic Wolfhound

The Irish Wolfhound is a breed of remarkable stature and legacy. As the tallest dog breed in the world, the Wolfhound can stand nearly three feet tall at the shoulder. Historically known as "cú faoil," these dogs were the prized war-hounds of Gaelic nobility. Their ownership was restricted to kings and chiefs, and they were often given as diplomatic gifts to foreign royalty. The legendary warrior Fionn mac Cumhaill was said to have owned over 300 of these hounds, including his favorites, Bran and Sceolan.

According to legend, these two hounds were not just dogs; they were Fionn's nephews, transformed into dogs by a rival of their mother.

The Wolfhound's history is deeply intertwined with Ireland's. In the 17th century, the British government in Ireland, led by Cromwell, even issued a decree to prevent the export of these "wolfe dogges," as large numbers of them were needed to control the wolf population. However, once wolves became extinct in the 18th century, the Wolfhound itself nearly vanished. Thankfully, in the 1860s, a dedicated effort led by Captain George Augustus Graham revived the breed through careful cross breeding.

The breed has since become an iconic symbol of Ireland. Nineteenth-century nationalist leader Daniel O'Connell was often painted with a large hunting dog to signify his ties to ancient Gaelic nobility. The Wolfhound is also a prominent symbol in Irish folklore and art. One tale recount how St. Patrick's blessing calmed a pagan prince's wolfhound, leading to the prince's conversion. Today, the Irish Wolfhound embodies the nation's spirit: gentle and friendly, but with a fierce and unforgettable history. This legacy continues at places like Ashford Castle Hotel in County Mayo, where resident wolfhounds often greet guests, acting as living mascots who embody the breed's gentle and majestic nature.

The Faithful Terriers

Irish Terrier

Often called the "Daredevil" of terriers, the Irish Terrier is a breed with a fiery personality and a heart as bold as any wolfhound. With its distinctive wiry red coat, this breed originated as an all-purpose farm dog, earning a reputation as a fearless vermin hunter. By the late 19th century, its spirited character gained popularity at dog shows, making it one of the first terrier breeds to be formally recognized.

The modern breed's lineage can be traced back to a dog named Killiney Boy, a charming terrier from Dublin. His legacy was so significant that a prominent breeder, Mr. H. Waterhouse, ensured his genes were passed down to future generations. The Irish Terrier's popularity quickly spread beyond Ireland's borders. The breed was favored by European royalty, including the Austro-Hungarian Habsburgs, who used them as shooting dogs. They were also prized by the Rajahs and Maharajahs of British India. This international fame was underscored in 1903 when King Edward VII brought his Irish Terrier, Jack, on a state visit to Ireland. Jack's untimely death, shortly after his arrival in Ireland, led to his burial with full honors in Dublin's Phoenix Park, where a small headstone marks his grave.

The breed's courage was put to the test in World War I, where they were employed as messenger dogs in the trenches. Their agility and bravery under fire saved countless lives, earning them the nickname "Micks" from the troops. One famous Irish Terrier, "Paddy," delivered a crucial message despite being gassed and wounded, collapsing only after completing his mission. Another Irish terrier belonging to the American forces, named Goldberg, was gassed and severely wounded by shrapnel but survived the war. Upon his death, his body was preserved and is now housed in the Illinois State Military Museum, a testament to his service. The breed's loyalty and courage are captured in the old Irish saying that an Irish Terrier "would follow you to the gates of hell and snarl at the devil himself."

Kerry Blue Terrier

The Kerry Blue Terrier (Irish: An Brocaire Gorm) is a breed as distinctive in its looks as in its lore. Hailing from County Kerry, this terrier was a true jack-of-all-trades on the Irish farm, used for hunting vermin, herding livestock, and guarding the homestead. What makes the breed truly unique is its coat, which is black at birth and gradually fades to a slate blue as the dog matures. This magical color change inspired a legend that the breed originated from a mysterious blue dog that swam ashore from a Spanish Armada shipwreck in 1588 and mated with local terriers.

By the 1920s, the Kerry Blue had become a powerful symbol of Irish pride. The revolutionary leader Michael Collins was a passionate advocate for the breed. Despite being a wanted man with a £10,000 bounty on his head, Collins famously hid in plain sight, even attending a Dublin dog show under an alias to enter his own Kerry Blue, Convict 224, a name that cheekily referenced the prison number of his then ally, Éamonn de Valera. Collins intended to have the Kerry Blue declared the national dog of the Irish Free State, a plan that was tragically cut short by his death in 1922. The breed remains an icon of Irish heritage.

While Michael Collins was making the Kerry Blue Terrier a symbol of Irish rebellion, the family of writer Samuel Beckett also developed a deep affection for the breed. Beckett's mother, May Beckett, was a reserved woman who showed an open love for her dogs that she often denied to her sons. The family owned several Kerry Blues, and Samuel himself became particularly attached to a bitch named Wolf. This bond was so strong that when his mother had the dog euthanized to spare his feelings while he was away, Beckett fell into a deep depression.

The Kerry Blue is as beloved for its lively and mischievous personality as it is for its history. The breed is known for its intelligence, and like a cat, it is a naturally clean animal that takes care of its own coat. They make for alert watchdogs and devoted family pets, being gentle with children but always ready for an adventure. Today, if you visit the town of Listowel in County Kerry, you can see a statue of a Kerry Blue Terrier, a fitting tribute to the county's famous native.

Soft-Coated Wheaten Terrier

The Soft-Coated Wheaten Terrier, a breed with a silky, golden coat and a cheerful disposition, has its roots as a versatile farm dog in rural Ireland. For over two hundred years, Wheatens were the all-purpose dogs of small farmers, earning them the affectionate nickname "the poor man's Wolfhound" since peasants were legally forbidden from owning the large, valuable hounds of the aristocracy. These adaptable terriers performed a variety of tasks, from hunting vermin and herding livestock to guarding the homestead. A few were even said to have been trained to turn a spit for roasting meat in a kitchen treadwheel.

Despite their humble origins, Wheatens were highly cherished. They were known to snuggle in bed with children on cold nights. Their happy and people-oriented nature is so well-known that their enthusiastic jump and hug when greeting someone is affectionately called the "Wheaten Greeting." Like the Kerry Blue Terrier, Wheaten puppies are often born with a dark coat that gradually fades to their characteristic wheaten-gold color as they mature. The breed was officially recognized by the Irish Kennel Club in 1937 and has since grown in popularity worldwide, partly due to its hypoallergenic, low-shedding coat.

Glen of Imaal Terrier

The Glen of Imaal Terrier is a tough, low-to-the-ground breed that hails from the remote Glen of Imaal in County Wicklow. Nicknamed the

"Glen," this terrier is built like a big dog on short legs, with a muscular frame and strong hindquarters that were developed for digging. Its origins are debated, with some believing the breed was created when French and Hessian mercenary soldiers settled in the area in the 16th century, bringing with them a type of dwarf basset hound that they cross-bred with local terriers. Other accounts suggest the breed was introduced by Huguenot immigrants who came to Ireland to escape oppression.

The Glen of Imaal Terrier's value was in its utility. It was an all-purpose farm dog, hunting rats, foxes, and badgers, sometimes even going into burrows to fight prey larger than itself. Their silent and stoic temperament made them ideal for hunting and guarding. Historically, Glens were required to pass a "Certificate of Courage" by silently drawing a badger from its underground home or sett within a specific time. Thankfully, these trials were banned in 1966.

Despite its hard-working nature, the Glen of Imaal Terrier remained largely unknown outside of its home region and was slow to gain recognition. It was not officially recognized by the Irish Kennel Club until 1934. The breed is the antithesis of a pampered lapdog and is known for its calm and gentle demeanor. Today, the Glen of Imaal Terrier is still a relatively rare breed but is cherished for its loyalty, courage, and endearing character.

Sporting Setters and Spaniels

Irish Red and White Setter

The Irish Red and White Setter is a breed with a long and fascinating history. It is the older of the two Irish Setter breeds, with roots dating back to the 17th century. Irish hunters of the era favored these setters for their distinctive dual-colored coats, which made them easy to spot against the backdrop of fields and moors. Their work was vital to hunters, as they would range out to find game birds and point to their location.

By the 1800s, however, a shift in fashion toward the solid red setters led to a decline in the population of the Red and Whites. By the early 20th century, the breed was nearly extinct. The Red and White Setter owes its survival to a few dedicated individuals, most notably Reverend Noble Houston, who began a breeding program in the 1920s to save the breed from vanishing. His efforts paid off, and the breed was eventually granted full recognition as a separate breed in 1980 by the Irish Kennel Club.

The Irish Red and White Setter is known for its affectionate nature and energetic personality. They are slightly shorter and more robust than their solid-red cousins. Their temperament is described as methodical and loyal, often working closely with their owners. These qualities, along with their unique and striking appearance, make them a beloved but still relatively uncommon breed today.

Irish Red Setter

The Irish Red Setter, with its iconic mahogany-red coat, is one of Ireland's most recognizable dog breeds. The breed is a descendant of the older Irish Red and White Setter, with its stunning solid-red coat becoming the favored standard in the 19th century. The Irish Red Setter Club, one of the first of its kind, was established in Dublin in 1882 to promote the breed.

These dogs are known for their high energy, intelligence, and affectionate nature, making them a family favorite. The breed has captured the hearts of many, including Irish nationalist leader Charles Stewart Parnell, who famously insisted that his faithful Red Setter remain by his side as he was on his deathbed.

Irish Water Spaniel

The Irish Water Spaniel, often called the "Clown of the Bog," is a breed with a distinct appearance and a long history as a water retriever. Believed to be one of Ireland's oldest native breeds, its modern form was largely established in the 1800s by a Dublin sportsman named Justin McCarthy and his legendary dog, Boatswain, who is credited as the progenitor of the breed. This spaniel is instantly recognizable by its dense liver-colored curls and a smooth, hairless "rat tail." Its unique physique, including webbed feet, makes it an excellent swimmer and well-suited to retrieving waterfowl.

The breed has an endearing and comical personality, earning it the nickname "clown of the spaniel family." Their playful nature and characteristic topknot of longer curls give them a perpetually quizzical and humorous expression. Despite their goofy demeanor, they are intelligent and highly skilled gun dogs. A writer in the 1870s noted that the Irish Water Spaniel was a perfect "canine one-stop shop" for gentlemen of limited means, as it could perform the duties of a pointer, setter, and retriever all in one.

Throughout history, the Irish Water Spaniel was a valuable working dog and even a diplomatic gift from one leader to another. In the 17th century, a "smooth tailed" spaniel from Ireland was reportedly given to the King of France by King James of England to improve relations between the two countries. Today, this unique breed is relatively rare but is cherished by enthusiasts for its versatile skills, intelligence, and playful nature.

The Enduring Kerry Beagle

The Kerry Beagle is one of Ireland's oldest hound breeds, a sleek scenthound with a rich history. Despite its name, it is not a beagle, but a larger hound, and its origins are debated. Some folklore suggests the breed descended from a dog that swam ashore from a Spanish Armada shipwreck or arrived with French traders in the 17th century. Others believe the Kerry Beagle may be a remnant of ancient Celtic hounds. A more fanciful legend claims the breed's ancestors were two hounds that escaped Noah's Ark as it passed over Ireland.

Regardless of its true origin, the Kerry Beagle has a long history as a working hunter, particularly for stag and fox. Its name is thought to come from the Irish word "beag," meaning "small," perhaps to differentiate it from larger hounds. The breed's stamina and highly developed sense of smell made it an invaluable partner, often working with larger dogs like the Irish Wolfhound. The Kerry Beagle's endurance is legendary, and some packs, such as the famous Scarteen Hounds of County Limerick, have been hunting continuously for over 300 years. It was from these hounds that the British counter-insurgency force in the Irish War of Independence, who wore a mix of khaki and rifle green, acquired the nickname "Black and Tans."

Today, the Kerry Beagle is a rare breed, even in Ireland. For most of its history, it was kept by dedicated hunting families rather than as a pet or show dog. However, in recent decades, it has gained a small following as a companion animal. Though it needs plenty of exercise, the Kerry Beagle is known for its gentle, friendly nature at home. This breed, which has weathered centuries of change and turmoil, serves as a powerful symbol of Ireland's enduring heritage.

Dog Heroes

In modern Ireland, several dogs have achieved fame for their heroic actions and remarkable deeds. Here are just a few of their stories.

Mick the Miller—The Racing Champion:

Born in County Offaly in 1926, Mick the Miller became the first true superstar of greyhound racing. His incredible speed and charisma made him a household name. He made history by winning the English Greyhound Derby in both 1929 and 1930, a feat that had never been accomplished before. Mick was so popular that he even starred as himself in a 1934 film. When he passed away in 1939, his funeral was attended by large crowds, and he is remembered today as the "grandfather of greyhound racing." A bronze statue now honors his memory in his hometown of Killeigh.

Hunter—The Gardaí's Top Dog:

Hunter, a skilled German Shepherd serving with Ireland's police force, the Gardaí, proved the vital role of police dogs in modern crime fighting. In April 2020, during a routine traffic stop in north Dublin, a suspect attempted to escape on foot. Hunter quickly tracked the fugitive's scent through the streets, cornering the man and leading to his arrest. The police also recovered an expensive watch from the suspect, a detail that earned Hunter the humorous nickname of being a "watch dog" who helped seize a "watch."

Jack—The Rescue Who Rescued Back:

In December 2021, an elderly man named Pat Brennan was taking an evening walk near Portarlington, County Laois, when he fell into a ditch and was out of sight of potential rescuers. His newly adopted terrier pup, Jack, became his guardian angel. When emergency crews arrived, the little dog, only a year old, refused to leave his human. He waited by the roadside, drawing the attention of the rescuers and leading them directly to Pat. The previously stray dog, who had been rescued just six months earlier, became an internet sensation for his loyalty, proving that a rescued dog might just rescue you right back.

Wilbur—The Fire Alarm on Four Legs:

In 2022, a family in County Cork learned that heroes can come with fur and floppy ears. Wilbur, a one-year-old Rhodesian Ridgeback mix adopted from Dogs Trust Ireland, was known for his calm temperament. But when a fire broke out in the home, he sprang into action, barking frantically until his sleeping owners woke up. Thanks to Wilbur's urgent alarm, the family was able to escape the blaze unharmed. His quick thinking was credited with saving their lives. It just goes to show that even the gentlest of dogs can act with incredible courage when a loved one is in danger.

Rover—The Churchgoing Dog:

In the 1960s, a stray dog named Rover became a local legend in the village of Clogherhead, County Louth. A stray sheepdog mix, Rover adopted the village as his home around 1956 and soon began a remarkable routine. He would attend 7:30 a.m. Mass every Sunday without fail. By 1969, his devout habit had caught the attention of national news, with an RTÉ television news report marveling at his nine-year streak of church attendance.

Underdogs who Came Out on Top

Master McGrath: An Irish Racing Legend

Arguably the most famous Irish dog of the 19th century, Master McGrath was a greyhound who rose from humble beginnings to become an international superstar. As a puppy, he was the runt of his litter and was nearly drowned on his owner's orders, but a local farm boy saved him. Master McGrath went on to dominate the sport, becoming the first dog ever to win England's prestigious Waterloo Cup three times between 1868 and 1871. Nicknamed "the immortal black," he lost only one of his 37 races. His fame was so great that even Queen Victoria requested a private presentation to see the champion hound. Master McGrath's story is a true rags-to-riches tale of a little black pup who defied all odds to become the pride of Ireland's dog racing history.

Kim the Jack Russell: A Roscommon Legal Drama

In 2022, a County Roscommon Jack Russell named Kim became the focus of a legal and public drama. After an incident in which she bit a passerby, a court initially ordered that the dog be put down. For Kim's elderly owner, 79-year-old Donal Rogers, the prospect was devastating — Kim was his constant companion. Rogers walked her every day, fed her a variety of meals, and gave her treats, and was deeply bonded with the Jack Russell.

The case struck a chord across Ireland. A widespread "Save Kim" campaign ignited, with an online petition collecting more than 176,000 signatures and drawing coverage from national and international media. Supporters recognized that for Rogers, losing Kim would mean far more than the loss of a pet. It would mean the loss of his main source of companionship and comfort in old age, a blow that would have left him isolated and heartbroken.

In October 2022, a judge issued a compassionate ruling that overturned the destruction order. Instead, Kim was allowed to remain with Rogers under strict safety restrictions, ensuring that nobody else would be bitten by the feisty fellow.

Modern-Day Doggies

Breed Clubs

Organized breed clubs and enthusiastic fanciers are central to Ireland's canine heritage today. These groups work to preserve the nine breeds recognized as indigenous to Ireland by the Irish Kennel Club, including the Irish Wolfhound, Irish Terrier, Kerry Blue, Soft-Coated Wheaten, Glen of Imaal, Irish Red and White Setter, Irish Red Setter, Irish Water Spaniel, and Kerry Beagle.

The efforts of these clubs ensure that Ireland's dog breeds not only survive but also thrive. The Irish Wolfhound Club, for instance, organizes annual "Wolfhound Walks" at historic sites, and the Irish Terrier Club, founded in 1896, maintains a rescue network. The Dublin Blue Terrier Club, co-founded by Michael Collins in 1920, still exists today as a living link to Irish history.

These organizations also play a crucial role in promoting the breeds. They lobby for heritage status for native breeds, hold public showcases, and even march in St. Patrick's Day parades. At some dog shows, a tradition has emerged where the national anthem is sung during a parade of Irish breeds, with a few wolfhounds rumored to howl along. Today, there are also non-pedigree clubs for working sheepdogs, showcasing their herding skills in annual competitions.

The origins of these organizations date back to the 19th century, with the establishment of societies for the prevention of cruelty to animals in Belfast in 1836 and Dublin in 1840. This era also saw the rise of pioneers who championed specific breeds, such as Lord Rossmore for the Red and White Setter and Justin McCarthy for the Irish Water Spaniel. In 1922, a genuinely independent Irish Kennel Club was formed, separate from the British Kennel Club, giving it the authority to set and recognize its own breed standards and ensuring that Ireland's rich variety of dogs are not lost to time.

Rescue Networks

The Irish dog rescue community is a powerful force for good. In the Republic of Ireland, there are over 100 volunteer-run dog rescues in addition to roughly 30 county shelters. Well-known organizations like Dogs Trust Ireland, the ISPCA, and MADRA (Mutts Anonymous Dog Rescue and Adoption. "Madra" also means dog in Irish) work alongside smaller groups and breed-specific rescues, such as Irish Retriever Rescue and Greyhound Rescue Association Ireland. This network of organizations collaborates informally, often transporting dogs across the country to find them a spot in a shelter or foster home with available capacity. A heartwarming example of this cooperation occurred in 2018 when a shelter in Cavan was overwhelmed with abandoned collie pups, and a rescue in Dublin organized a "collie convoy" to find them homes in the capital.

Advocacy and Social Media

Social media has been a game-changer for rescue efforts in Ireland, with online groups helping to reunite lost pets and connect potential adopters with shelters. The community response to appeals for help is often incredible, with people donating money, food, and blankets, and offering to provide foster homes. The rescue community is also leading a growing movement against puppy farming and campaigning for stronger animal welfare laws. Activists have successfully pressured the government to tighten breeding regulations, and the message to "Adopt, Don't Shop!" is a constant refrain. As of 2023, approximately 3,200 dogs were in Irish shelters at any given time, and rescuers are determined to reduce that number.

These efforts extend internationally, with many retired Irish racing greyhounds finding loving homes abroad thanks to partnerships with organizations in the UK, Italy, and the US. The dedication of Ireland's rescue network is a bright light, saving one dog at a time. As one rescue's slogan aptly says, "Saving one dog won't change the world, but for that one dog, the world will change forever."

Therapy Programs

In recent years, Ireland has embraced the power of therapy dogs, which are bringing comfort and joy to people in hospitals, schools, and care homes. A pioneering group, Irish Therapy Dogs, trains and registers volunteer dog-and-owner teams who make weekly visits to nursing homes, hospices, and hospitals. The sight of a gentle Golden Retriever or a friendly Collie can invariably bring smiles and spark conversations, helping to break through loneliness and provide devoted companionship. Residents who may be struggling with memory or mood often light up, recalling pets from their past or simply enjoying the tactile comfort of stroking a dog's fur.

Another innovative initiative is the School Therapy Dog Programme, which places calm, trained dogs in classrooms, particularly to support children with autism or anxiety. These dogs help students feel at ease and can encourage a child who is too anxious to read aloud to read confidently to a patient dog. Even Irish universities have brought in therapy dogs to help students de-stress during exam weeks. Irish hospitals like Tallaght and Galway also allow therapy dog visits in certain wards, where a wagging tail can help brighten a long recovery.

The organization Dogs for the Disabled Ireland also trains assistance dogs to perform tasks for people with physical disabilities, with a subset of dogs working as therapy companions for children with special needs. One moving story tells of a boy with severe autism who was non-verbal but began talking in simple phrases to his assistance dog, a Labrador named Fionn. The dog's steady, loving presence opened up the child's world and facilitated his first real communication. Such tales underline why therapy and service dogs are so highly valued.

Doggie Events

Ireland's love for dogs is evident in its lively dog-friendly events and festivals held throughout the year. From large-scale festivals to small-town shows, these events create a strong sense of community for both humans and canines.

Major Festivals

- **Pups in the Park:** This large touring festival takes place in Dublin (Marlay Park) and Cork (Cork showgrounds) and is a canine carnival with thousands of dogs and owners. It features activities like agility course try-outs, expert talks, doggy swimming pools, and costume contests.

- **Dogitude:** A two-day festival held at Causey Farm in County Meath, Dogitude celebrates everything dog related. It includes demonstrations of exciting canine sports like flyball and dock diving, along with workshops and fun activities like barn hunts and hay-bale mazes.

- **Barkfest:** This is a smaller, more relaxed festival in Kilkenny, often held in a pet-friendly café garden. It combines live music with dog-friendly activities and stalls from local businesses.

Shows and Competitions

- **Irish Kennel Club Championship Shows:** For serious dog enthusiasts, the IKC holds several championships shows annually. Dates vary by year; the main show is often in late summer or autumn. These events are a great opportunity to see top examples of various breeds, including rare Irish breeds, and to speak with breeders.

- **Sheepdog Trials:** These events, typically held during summer and autumn months, like the annual trial in County Donegal, are not pedigree-based but rather showcase the incredible herding skills of working dogs, most often Border Collies.

Charity and Community Events

- **Bark in the Park:** These are sponsored charity walks that take place in various cities, such as Dublin and Galway. They are organized to raise funds for the ISPCA and other local shelters.

- **Pet Expos:** Held in cities like Dublin, these events are part trade show and part expo. They feature stalls for dog products, training workshops, and areas where people can meet adoptable dogs from rescues.

- **Halloween "Howl-o-ween":** Many communities, including the Dublin SPCA, hold these events around late October. They often include costume contests and charity walks to raise funds.

- **St. Patrick's Day Dog Parades:** Some towns, like Belfast and Cork, include a special segment in their St. Patrick's Day parades for dogs in costume. In Cork, there was even a record attempt for the most dogs in a parade on St. Patrick's Day.

Teach your dog Irish

Why not sprinkle a bit of the Irish language into Fido's vocabulary? Many Irish dog owners enjoy using Gaeilge (Irish Gaelic) phrases as commands. Here are a few Irish dog commands (with phonetic pronunciation) to try with your pup.

- **Suigh síos** – *Sit down*. (Pronounced roughly "sih SHEE-uss"). Often just "Suigh!" ("Sit!") for short. Your dog might cock his head at the new word, but with consistency, "Suigh" can work as well as "Sit."

- **Fan** – *Stay/Wait*. (Pronounced "fahn" –). A handy command when you want your dog to hold still. You can say "Fan liom" ("Wait for me") if you want to be more specific.

- **Tar anseo** – *Come here*. (Pronounced "tahr on-SHUH"). Tar (come) on its own is pronounced like the English word "tar."

- **Labhair** – *Speak/Bark*. (Pronounced "LAU-ir," kind of like flower without the f). If you want to teach your dog to bark on cue, Labhair is the command for you.

- **Maith an cailín/buachaill** – *Good girl/boy*. ("Mah an colleen/Mah an boo-a-hill'") Often we just say "Maith thú!" – Good on you! – to praise a dog (pronounced "mah hoo"). It's a lovely positive reinforcement; dogs may not know Irish grammar, but they will definitely understand your appreciative tone.

There are even online videos and apps dedicated to teaching dogs Gaeilge. While your pup might not become fully bilingual, it's a great way to celebrate Ireland's language. Go on, try it – fan… suigh… maith thú! good dog.

Dog-Preneurs

Ireland's entrepreneurial spirit has gone to the dogs – literally – with a host of creative businesses catering to canine needs and whims. Dublin's Barkin' Bakery creates fresh, wholesome cakes and treats for dogs— pawfect for special occasions or simply to spoil a beloved pet with cupcakes and biscuits made from dog-friendly ingredients. For grooming needs, Ireland offers an impressive selection: Dial a Dog Wash provides a mobile service that brings award-winning grooming straight to your door, so dogs can enjoy stress-free washing outside the home in their specially equipped vans. Their team uses gentle, natural products and has won "Mobile Dog Groomer of the Year" two years running.

In the Dublin suburb of Terenure, Dogsbody Grooming Salon is one of the country's oldest and most reputable parlours, renowned for breed-specific styling, nail care, and personal attention from highly experienced groomers. Show dog handlers and everyday pet owners trust Dogsbody for its quality and compassion. Maxi Zoo stores nationwide offer professional salon services, from routine coat care to pampering spa treatments, making high-quality grooming accessible for dogs of all sizes and breeds.

For innovative dog accessories and lifestyle solutions, DogDry stands out as an Irish success story. Their super-absorbent, waterproof drying robes and travel beds protect pets and owners from wet messes after walks, swims, or rainy adventures—loved by customers for keeping cars and homes dry and comfortable. DogDry's products have been featured on Irish television and are popular among dog enthusiasts for their practicality and style.

And for those seeking trusted care providers, global apps like Rover and Trusted House Sitters connect Irish dog owners with vetted walkers and sitters—offering peace of mind and flexibility for busy lifestyles. Ireland's entrepreneurial dog culture is dynamic, creative, and truly devoted to making life better for four-legged family members, whether through tasty treats, spa-quality grooming, or clever home solutions.

Irish Dog Names from Mythology

Irish history and mythology are rich with heroic hounds and faithful furry friends. These traditional names come straight from legends, bestowing a heroic pedigree on any pup:

Bran (pronounced like "brawn") – In Irish mythology, Bran is one of the two famous hounds of Fionn Mac Cool, leader of the Fianna, a band of mythical heroes in ancient Irish mythology. The name means "raven," a nod to his dark fur and keen intelligence. A dog named Bran carries a noble air – after all, mythic Bran could outsmart supernatural foes and never left his master's side. Don't be surprised if your Bran is clever and a bit enigmatic, with a watchful gaze as if guarding ancient secrets.

Sceolan (pronounced SHK-K-YOH-lahn) – The sister to Bran in myth, Sceolan's name is said to mean "survivor" or "little protector." She was the other cherished hound of Fionn MacCool, described in old tales as swift and fearless. A Sceolan might surprise you with her bravery, whether it's fearlessly chasing off pigeons from the garden or "protecting" the household from the dreaded vacuum cleaner.

Ailbé (pronounced "AL-beh") – Ailbé is the legendary Irish Wolfhound of mythic proportions, famed for his ferocity, fidelity, and guarding prowess. In one tale, Ailbé defended an entire kingdom and even in death refused to let go of an enemy's chariot – talk about tenacity. Naming your dog Ailbé sets a high bar for courage and loyalty. Expect an Ailbé to be protective but gentle with family, the kind of dog who might bark at intruders (or the delivery man) yet snooze with a toddler curled up against him. With this ancient name, even a pint-sized terrier will feel like a warrior hound guarding the gates of Tara, the historical seat of the High Kings of Ireland and a symbol of ancient Irish power and national identity.

Fionn (pronounced "FYUN") – A name meaning "fair-haired" or "white" in Irish, Fionn immediately calls to mind the legendary Finn Mac Cool himself. It's a fitting choice for a pale-coated dog. Picture a lovely white Samoyed or a blond lab named Fionn. In Irish lore, Fionn was a wise warrior and hunter, and many a doggo named Fionn seems to have a wise, patient demeanor. The name has a friendly, breezy sound – easy to call across the fields. Give your dog this storied name and you might find yourself telling the old tales on your walks: of how Fionn gained his wisdom by tasting the Salmon of Knowledge, or how he led the Fianna. Just be prepared: a dog named Fionn might assume he's the leader of your household band of heroes (and who are we to argue?).

Irish-Language Dog Names (As Gaeilge - In Irish)

Many dog lovers are now turning to the Irish language itself for inspiration. Gaelic names can carry beautiful meanings and a musical lilt, celebrating Ireland's heritage. Here are a few Irish-language names (for both cailíní and buachaillí, girls and boys) that might suit your furry friend:

Saoirse *(SEER-sha)* – This popular Irish name means "freedom," and it's perfect for a high-spirited dog who zooms with wild abandon. Saoirse has become familiar worldwide (thanks in part to actress Saoirse Ronan). A dog named Saoirse is likely to embody joy and independence. She might love running off-lead on the beach, ears flying, ignoring your calls until she's had her fill of freedom. Yet when she returns, she'll collapse happily at your feet, free and utterly content. Training a Saoirse might require a sense of humor (all that free spirit!), but her affectionate nature and vivacity will win you over.

Oisín *(uh-SHEEN)* – In Irish, Oisín means "little deer," and it comes straight from mythology – Oisín was the son of Fionn MacCool, Ireland's most famous and bravest legendary warrior. Oisin was born of a woman who had been transformed into a deer. This name is ideal for a graceful, fleet-footed dog. Perhaps your whippet who springs like a fawn, or that mutt who delicately tiptoes around puddles has an inner Oisín. The name carries a poetic weight (Oisín was also a legendary poet). An Oisín in the dog park might be gentle with smaller pups and surprisingly wise in those deep, dark eyes. Don't be surprised if your Oisín loves the rustle of woods and autumn leaves – the call of the wild deer may run in his soul. Give him this name and every jaunt in nature becomes a little slice of Tír na nÓg, the land of eternal youth where Oisín once traveled.

Orla *(OR-lah)* – From the Irish Órlaith, meaning "golden princess," Orla is a lovely choice for a pampered female dog – or any pup with a coat shining like the sun. This name dates to medieval Ireland (it was borne by high king Brian Boru's sister, a princess), yet it feels fresh and easy to call. An Orla might have a bit of diva in her, expecting the finest treats and the coziest spot by the hearth (naturally, a princess has standards). But the name also implies warmth and regality without being too formal. Think of a dog who carries herself with gentle dignity, whether she's a rescue greyhound or a tiny Cavachon. With a meaning like "golden princess," don't be surprised if your Orla rules your heart and home in no time.

Fiadh *(FEE-ah)* – A top trending name in Ireland recently, Fiadh comes from the Irish word for "wild" or "wildlife," often associated with deer. Fiadh is perfect for a free-spirited girl dog whose queen of the back yard (and maybe escape artist in chief). Whether she's a russet-coated Irish setter or a feisty terrier mix, a Fiadh keeps you on your toes. One minute she's quietly observing butterflies, the next she's off through the fields in joyous abandon. But don't let "wild" fool you – Fiadhs are often deeply loving with their human pack. After an afternoon of adventures, your Fiadh will flop down, mud on her paws and a twinkle in her eye, as if to say, "Wasn't that grand?"

Dogs in the Tourist Industry

Ireland's tourism industry has discovered that dogs can be an attractive part of the package. For one, many tourist sites have resident dogs that are minor celebrities. At Ashford Castle Hotel in County Mayo, the two Irish Wolfhounds that greet guests each morning has become Instagram-famous attractions and guests line up for photos during the daily wolfhound walk on the grounds.

In Connemara, some tour companies offer sheepdog demonstration experiences. Visitors look on as a farmer's border collies herd sheep as the dogs respond to whistle commands from the farmer. Set against stunning mountain backdrops, these demos give tourists a taste of rural Irish life and have proven hugely popular, essentially turning working farm dogs into tourism ambassadors. And yes, everyone wants to pet the hardworking collie afterward!

Ireland is also marketing itself as a dog-friendly travel destination. Tourism Ireland's official site has a page on "Bringing your pet to Ireland," highlighting dog-friendly accommodations and trails. Indeed, more hotels and B&Bs across Ireland now advertise pet-friendly rooms. Some even provide dog beds and welcome treats – for example, several hotels in Kerry offer a "VIP (Very Important Pet) Package," including the Killeen House Hotel in Killarney. Even Ireland's tourism imagery has gone to the dogs. Marketing campaigns often show images of happy travelers hiking emerald hills with a trusty Irish Setter bounding ahead, or tourists enjoying a Guinness in a pub garden with a local sheepdog lying under the table.

The Wild Atlantic Way, Ireland's famous coastal route, sees many road-trippers with dogs in tow, so towns along the way have set up water bowls outside shops and designated dog-friendly dining spots, making it one of the most dog-friendly road trips in Europe.

The Wolfhound Experience offers a walking tour in Dublin's St. Stephen's Green area where you can have a personal encounter with a pack of Irish Wolfhounds and their "siblings" an Irish Setter and an Irish Terrier. On the 1.5-hour tour, you can learn about the history and mythology of the breed and take photos with the dogs, making it a unique option for tourists who love dogs and want a special experience in Dublin.

A Couple of Literary Dogs

Apart from holding a special place in Irish culture for centuries, as loyal companions and working animals, they've also featured as characters in literature. These canine characters are more than just background figures. They serve as mirrors to their human counterparts, reflecting social values, national identity, and the intricate bonds between people and their pets. The following two examples (my own personal favorites) showcase how Irish writers have used their four-legged friends to add depth, humor, and a touch of realism to their works.

Maria, the Mischief-Making Spaniel

In Somerville & Ross's classic collection of stories, the Irish R.M. series from the 1890s, one character constantly upstages the human cast, an unruly Irish Water Spaniel named Maria. From the perspective of the English narrator, Major Yeates and R.M, or resident magistrate, who is already bewildered by an Irish life, far removed from English norms, Maria is a constant source of both frustration and amusement. His wife had hoped their wedding-gift dog would follow the noble example of the legendary hound Gelert, being docile at home and brave in the field. Maria, however, had other plans.

The water spaniel was indeed a force to be reckoned with during a hunt, fearlessly chasing down game and even gobbling up birds her master shot. But around the house, she was a furry menace, sneaking leftovers from the dining table, damaging woodwork when punished, and even hiding food behind sofa cushions. Despite her antics—which included biting beggars and bullying, the servants—Major Yeates could never stay angry with the canine scamp for long. All it took was a hopeful glance or a paw placed on his knee, and every one of her transgressions was instantly forgiven. Maria's dramatic swings in personality, from a rambunctious buccaneer to a beguiling puppy, made her an endearing figure in late 19th-century Irish literature.

Garryowen – Joyce's Mongrel Satire

In his monumental novel Ulysses, James Joyce includes a portrait of a dog named Garryowen. Appearing in the "Cyclops" chapter, Garryowen is the canine companion of the ultra-nationalist character known as "the Citizen." The dog's name itself is a deliberate and ironic joke by Joyce. While it refers to a famous Irish rugby club and a traditional tune, it's also a nod to a real-life champion Irish Red Setter owned by one of Joyce's relatives.

Joyce initially presents Garryowen in an over-the-top, grandiose style, using epic language to describe him as a magnificent "wolf dog." This is a parody of the Celtic Revival, a movement that often-glorified ancient Irish mythology and heroes, and which Joyce viewed unfavorably. However, the unnamed narrator quickly exposes the sham, bluntly describing Garryowen as "a bloody mangy mongrel." The dog's dubious heritage and nasty disposition are a direct reflection of the Citizen's own exaggerated patriotism and deep-seated prejudices.

Songs

"Me Little Jack Russell"

"Me Little Jack Russell" is a humorous modern folk song by Irish comedian-songwriter Richie Kavanagh. In this upbeat ditty, Kavanagh affectionately describes a feisty Jack Russell terrier with a lively personality. The lyrics paint a comical portrait of the small dog's antics: "He was a little devil… he'd bark at the cat… [he'd be] waiting for the postman, he'd never let him past." Kavanagh's trademark wit shines through lines comparing the tiny pet's snarling to a "little shark." We're sure anyone who has a Jack Russell in their life can be related!

"Master McGrath"

"Master McGrath" is a classic 19th-century Irish ballad commemorating a legendary greyhound. Written around 1880 by James Custer, it honors the Irish dog Master McGrath, who famously won the Waterloo Cup coursing competition and became a national hero. The song's lyrics proudly celebrate Irish pride and the dog's triumph over English rivals. In one verse, Master McGrath retorts to a sneering Englishman, "we have wild heather bogs, but you'll find in old Ireland there's good men and dogs" and later raises his paw with the cry "Three cheers for old Ireland!"

"The Irish Rover"

"The Irish Rover" is a beloved song about a fantastical ship, known for its wildly improbable cargo and crew. Though most of the song is a comical tall tale, it concludes on a note of canine tragedy, at least in the version made famous by The Pogues, a Celtic punk band from the 1980s that fused traditional Irish folk music with punk rock. After a seven-year voyage, only the narrator and the captain's dog survive a measles outbreak, until the ship strikes a rock and capsizes, and "the poor aul dog was drowned," leaving the narrator as the sole survivor, "the last of the Irish Rover." This unexpected mention of the captain's loyal dog, lost in the shipwreck, adds a touch of bittersweet pathos to the rousing tune. The song (attributed to J. M. Crofts in the 1960s) has been recorded by numerous artists (notably The Dubliners and The Pogues) and remains a favorite in pub sing-songs.

"The Running Dog"

"The Running Dog" (also known as "Murphy's Running Dog") is a century-old Wexford folk song often performed by singer Paddy Berry.

Written by local man Michael O'Brien around the turn of the 20th century, it celebrates a greyhound known as "The Juggler," owned by the Murphy family of Ballykerogue. The song has a playful, humorous tone as it recounts the dog's energetic racing adventures across Ireland and the owner's misadventures in betting. In the lyrics, the spirited hound wins some races but comically "lost the race when he stopped to lick his paw" mid-chase. The chorus bemoans the owner's gambling losses but cheers the dog's enthusiasm.

The Irish Pug Song (Loca the Pug)

"The Irish Pug Song" is a viral comedic song that charmed the internet with the story of a little pug who "can't feckin' run." The star of the song is Loca, a special needs pug from Belfast, whose owners created this light-hearted tune about her inability to run properly. Set to a bouncing Irish-style rhythm, the lyrics (sung in an Irish accent) introduce Loca: "Well, hello, my name is Loca and I'm a special pug, I live in Belfast, Ireland…" and humorously catalog her attempts to chase birds and dogs despite her coordination problem. The chorus's memorable refrain – "I can't feckin' run" – is delivered with tongue-in-cheek frustration, making listeners laugh while sympathizing with the lovable dog. Fast-paced and irresistibly catchy, the song became an instant hit on social media around 2012, accumulating millions of views.

TV and Films

The President's Puppy Steals the Spotlight

A recent real-life viral moment proved that in Ireland, even the highest office isn't safe from canine mischief. In May 2021, the Irish President Michael D. Higgins was giving a solemn live TV interview at Áras an Uachtaráin (the presidential residence) when his Bernese Mountain Dog Misneach (the Irish word for courage) decided it was playtime. The 7-month-old pup pawed insistently at the President, gnawing on his hand and tugging at his jacket sleeve, all on-camera during the official broadcast. Higgins, who is a noted dog lover, gently tried to calm Misneach and even held the puppy's paw for a moment while gamely continuing his remarks. The sight of Ireland's head of state maintaining presidential composure as his huge fluffy puppy demanded attention was adorable and instantly went viral.

"Róise & Frank" – Canine Reincarnation

In the Irish-language film Róise & Frank (2022), a grieving widow finds new hope in an unlikely visitor, a stray dog she becomes convinced is the reincarnation of her late husband. At first, Róise is depressed and withdrawn after her husband Frank's death until a shaggy mutt appears on her doorstep and quickly integrates himself into the family. The dog somehow knows Frank's old routines, immediately curling up in Frank's favorite armchair and even leading Róise along her husband's habitual walking route. A vet happens to mention the dog is about two years old, the same length of time since Frank died, confirming Róise's suspicion that her beloved spouse's spirit lives on in her newly-found canine companion. The widow lovingly names the dog "Frank," after her husband, cooks it steak, and regains her zest for life (putting on makeup and rejoining the community). The gentle comedy takes a magical turn as "Frank" the dog starts performing little miracles around the village, like a furry guardian angel helping neighbors in need, which wins him many fans.

"Man About Dog" – A Greyhound Caper

This 2004 Irish comedy film is a rollicking tale of three clueless young men and a greyhound. Owing €50,000 to an unforgiving bookie, our trio agree to rig a dog race in exchange for a greyhound only to discover the dog (promptly named Boots) is utterly useless on the track. Scrambling for a Plan B, they acquire a second greyhound, the magnificently named Cerberus (after the three-headed dog who guarded the underworld in Greek mythology), and enter him in a big race…where he promptly lies down in the starting box and refuses to run, losing them even more money. Things go from bad to worse (the lads get kidnapped by the furious bookie), and soon they're on the run across Ireland with the non-running greyhound in tow. This leads to some madcap misadventures – including a chaotic high-speed van chase. Without spoiling the whole plot, let's say every underdog has his day: the heroes find out Cerberus will chase a real hare when it counts, and a once "useless" dog just might turn out to be their unexpected savior.

Instagram

Hashtags like #DogsOfIreland showcase daily Irish dog life from Giant's Causeway to Dublin city., very wholesome content. The trend shows that Irish dogs are as social media savvy as any, or rather their owners are! Scroll through Instagram and you'll find plenty of Irish dogs capturing hearts one post at a time. There's something about those green fields and windswept beaches that makes a perfect backdrop for photogenic pups.

Irish rescue organizations also leverage Instagram, posting "glamour shots" of adoptable dogs against scenic Irish locales. Who could resist a plea like "Meet Seamus, looking for his forever home!" with Seamus posed in front of the Cliffs of Moher.

However, one of the biggest accounts is actually run by an Irishman abroad: @niall.harbison chronicles an Irish entrepreneur's mission to save street dogs in Thailand. His videos of feeding and rehabilitating strays have gained over a million followers, proving uplifting dog content knows no borders.

Also worth checking out is "Ginormous Chicken" (@ginormouschicken), the tongue-in-cheek handle of an Irish Wolfhound living in the U.S. whose owner is Irish – this gentle giant "Chicken" has tens of thousands of followers who adore seeing him be an emotional support buddy to foster kittens and more.

Celebrities

Celebrities – they're just like us in their adoration of dogs, and Irish celebrities are no exception. Among actors, Colin Farrell has a soft spot for rescue dogs. He's often photographed walking his two adopted terrier mixes around Dublin and has used his platform to encourage adoption of strays.

The Science of "Finding Home"

Dogs possess a remarkable combination of senses that they use to get back to familiar territory. One key factor is their sense of smell. A dog's nose is thousands of times more sensitive than a human's, allowing them to pick up on familiar scents from miles away, creating a mental "scent map" of their surroundings. Another, more mysterious ability is their use of the Earth's geomagnetic field. Research suggests that dogs, like some other animals, may have the ability to sense the planet's magnetic field. This allows them to orient themselves and determine direction, even in unfamiliar terrain.

Mali – Arranmore Island, Donegal (2024)

In August 2024, Mali, a Bernese Mountain Dog, vanished on Arranmore Island, Donegal, after being spooked by a gale. After two weeks of searching by her German owners and the local community, a fishing boat crew heard her faint barks from a narrow cliff ledge 200 feet above the sea. Rescuers scaled the cliff to find Mali alive and well, her leash snagged on a rock. She was reunited with her family at the harbor just before they were scheduled to return home.

Baya – Athenry, Galway (2023)

Baya, a French Bulldog, disappeared from her home in Athenry, Galway, two years ago. In late 2023, the DSPCA (Dublin Society for the Prevention of Cruelty to Animals) found a lost Frenchie whose microchip scan revealed her long-lost family. Baya was reunited with her emotional owner, a bit older but safe and sound.

Neesha – Wicklow Mountains (2021)

Neesha, a Golden Retriever, got lost in the Wicklow Mountains after chasing a deer. For two weeks, the dog survived alone until two hiking doctors spotted her on a snowy peak. They wrapped the weak dog in their coats, and one carried her 10 kilometers down the mountain. She was then tearfully reunited with her family.

Buddy – Kerry (2018)

In 2018, Buddy the dog vanished in the Maharees dunes of County Kerry. For six long months, his family and the community searched tirelessly, even using drones. Buddy was finally found alive in October, sparking celebrations across the parish and proving the strength of the community and the bond between a family and their dog.

Irish Dogs - Facts and Figures

The Irish have long had a reputation as a nation of dog lovers, and recent statistics confirm this. Nearly 60% of Irish households own some type of pet, with dogs being the clear favorite. While older data from 2007 suggested a dog ownership rate of around 36%, more recent analyses confirm dogs are the most popular pet in Ireland, with studies indicating that up to 77% of households with multiple pets own at least one dog. Rural households are still more likely to own a dog than those in urban centers like Dublin, where roughly a quarter of households have a dog.

The most popular dog breeds in Ireland reflect a preference for both family-friendly companions and working dogs. The Labrador Retriever and Golden Retriever consistently rank at the top, along with the Jack Russell Terrier, known for its spirited personality.

Legal Requirements for Dog Owners

Modern Ireland has clear and progressive laws for dog ownership, which help ensure the safety and welfare of the country's canine population.

Microchipping and Registration: As of 2015, it is a legal requirement for all dogs to be microchipped and registered on a government-approved database. This must be done by the time a puppy is 12 weeks old, or before a change in ownership, whichever comes first. This law has been crucial in reuniting lost dogs with their owners and tackling illegal breeding.

Dog Licenses: A tradition carried over from the Victorian era, dog licenses are still a legal requirement in Ireland. All dogs over four months old must have a license, which can be purchased annually (€20), or for the dog's lifetime (140). This system helps local authorities fund dog control and welfare.

Travel to Ireland with Your Dog

Dreaming of exploring the Emerald Isle with your furry best friend? Good news: it's quite doable, with a bit of planning. Ireland (as part of the EU pet travel scheme) welcomes pet dogs if they meet certain requirements. If you're coming from abroad, your dog will need to be microchipped and have a valid rabies vaccination, plus an EU Pet Passport or official health certificate if from outside the EU. Also, dogs coming from many countries (like the USA or UK) must get a tapeworm treatment 1–5 days before entry (Ireland is tapeworm-free). There's no quarantine for pets that meet the rules, and they can step off the plane or ferry and start sniffing Irish soil right away.

Once here, you'll find that many accommodations are dog-friendly, but it's always wise to check in advance. There are charming rural B&Bs that allow dogs (some even have resident dogs eager to play), and a growing number of hotels in cities like Dublin, Galway, and Cork offer pet-friendly rooms. For example, the Westport Coast Hotel in County Mayo greets canine guests with a little welcome pack (toys and treats) and maps of local dog-walking sports – talk about céad míle fáilte!

Do keep in mind that dogs are not allowed in certain places like inside most restaurants, grocery stores, and some public transport, except for service dogs. However, outdoor seating at pubs and cafes is generally fine, and it's not unusual on a sunny day to see pub beer gardens dotted with snoozing dogs while owners enjoy a pint. Ireland's parks are a delight for dogs: Phoenix Park in Dublin is huge and dog-friendly (on leash in most areas), and many beaches allow dogs, especially outside of peak summer hours (some require a leash or have dog zones). Always check local signage, as each county can have its own bylaws about beach access – e.g., some popular beaches ask for leashes during bathing season but are off-leash heaven in mornings or off-season.

When traveling around, if you rent a car, it's easy – just ensure your dog is secured (many bring a crate or seat-belt harness). Trains in Ireland officially permit small dogs in carriers, and larger dogs at the discretion of staff – in practice, many people do take dogs on intercity trains, ideally at off-peak times and on leash/muzzle if required. Buses are trickier (generally not dog-friendly except service dogs). One great option: Ireland has several companies offering guided walking tours where dogs are explicitly welcome – think hiking the Wicklow Way or strolling the Burren with your pup by your side. Finally, a quirky travel tip: a few tourist attractions have kennels on site! The Cliffs of Moher Visitor Centre, for instance, doesn't allow dogs on the cliff paths for safety, but provides free kennel space while you visit (first come, first served).

Overall, Ireland can be a fantastic place to adventure with your dog. The key is to be prepared with paperwork and polite with Leave No Trace and leash etiquette. Do that, and you and your canine pal will receive the classic Irish hospitality – perhaps even an admiring "What a lovely dog!" from locals in whatever village pub you wander into. Slán sábhálta – safe travels – to you and your pup!

The Future of Irish Dogs

A New Era of Canine Compassion:

In Ireland, the movement toward better animal welfare is gaining steady ground. Recent reforms like mandatory microchipping, tighter puppy farm regulations, and updates to the Animal Health and Welfare Act signal a national commitment to treating dogs not just as property, but as sentient companions deserving of compassion. Rescue organizations, once scrappy grassroots efforts, are now networked, professionalized, and often partnered with international rehoming programs. The phrase "adopt, don't shop" is increasingly common across Irish social media feeds.

Revival and Pride in Native Breeds:

From the towering Irish Wolfhound to the tenacious Glen of Imaal Terrier, Ireland's nine native breeds are experiencing a passionate renaissance. Breed clubs and heritage advocates are leading the charge for increased awareness, responsible breeding, and international recognition. The Irish Kennel Club (IKC) has taken up the banner with targeted educational campaigns, showcasing breeds like the Irish Red Setter, the Kerry Blue Terrier, and the Irish Water Spaniel at events and on social media. Specific organizations, such as the Irish Wolfhound Club of Ireland, work tirelessly to protect their breed's lineage. There is also growing discussion around establishing dedicated heritage trails or museum exhibits to highlight these dogs as living cultural artifacts. This renewed focus is breathing new life into these historic breeds, which are now being celebrated not just as pets, but as cherished symbols of Irish heritage both at home and abroad.

Homegrown Grub:

Innovative Irish startups are emerging to serve modern dog owners, blending commerce with a love for animals. This growing sector offers everything from artisan dog food to natural pet treats crafted with local ingredients. For example, Bia Amh, based in Ireland, produces high-quality raw dog food made from Irish-sourced meats and vegetables that promote shinier coats and healthier skin. Meanwhile, Carnivore Kelly's, headquartered in Dublin with a family history in butchery, specializes in raw pet nutrition and offers subscription boxes of nutritionally complete raw diets delivered nationwide. For natural, handmade dog treats, small Irish businesses such as Harry's Dog Bakery are dedicated to slow-baked recipes using wholesome ingredients, delighting discerning canine customers. Together, these companies exemplify the vibrant and innovative spirit of Ireland's pet care industry, combining tradition and technology for the benefit of dogs and their owners alike

Meanwhile, app-based dog-walking and pet-sitting networks are active across the country, making it easy for owners to connect with trusted caregivers. International platforms like Rover and local services are widely used in cities like Dublin and Galway. Additionally, veterinary telehealth is expanding, with services such as Vet-On-Call providing a vital service that improves access to expert pet care, particularly in remote rural communities.

A Voice in the Courts—and the Dáil (Irish parliament)

Advocacy for stricter penalties on animal cruelty and tighter control on dangerous breeding practices continues to gain momentum. Legal experts and welfare charities are pressing for the full recognition of animals as sentient beings in Irish law, a concept already enacted in some EU countries. Irish courts are increasingly sympathetic in animal cruelty cases, and the political will is growing for updated, enforceable legislation—especially following high-profile cases of abuse or attacks.

Currency, Commerce, and China

The Irish sixpence coin, featuring the Irish wolfhound, was a particularly significant and long-lasting representation. The design, created by English artist Percy Metcalfe, was on the coin from 1928 until 1969. While the coin's design was clearly intended to be a wolfhound, a popular, unverified theory suggests the dog's inspiration may have been Master McGrath, a famous racing greyhound from County Waterford.

Brandy Dog Food is a well-established and beloved pet food brand with a rich heritage dating back to 1972. Founded in County Armagh, Northern Ireland, by John Mackle Sr., Brandy has grown from a small family business into one of the leading pet food manufacturers on the island of Ireland. The brand is instantly recognizable by its iconic packaging featuring Benson, a Bernese Mountain Dog, who has been the cheerful mascot for over 50 years, symbolizing the company's commitment to quality and loyalty. Operating under Mackle Petfoods, the company employs over 250 people across multiple production sites, reflecting its significant growth and presence in the market. Brandy Dog Food prides itself on using 100% locally sourced Irish meats, ensuring top-quality nutrition for dogs while supporting Irish farmers. The brand's product range respects tradition while embracing innovation, offering everything from budget-friendly everyday meals to premium ranges like Naturo, as well as modern freeze-dried snacks for health-conscious pet owners.

Historical Advertising:

The Irish Red Setter on the advertising for Spillane's Garryowen Plug tobacco was not just any dog; it was a champion show dog named Garryowen. The dog's fame was so widespread that he was even alluded to in James Joyce's Ulysses and received an obituary in the Chicago Tribune. This demonstrates how a well-known, prized dog could become a powerful marketing tool.

The Rabies Public Information Campaign:

In the late 1970s, facing a rabies threat from continental Europe, the Irish government and Bord Fáilte, the Irish Tourist Board, launched a major public information campaign. The TV ads were dramatic, with a stark message: "Rabies kills. Don't let it happen here. Don't bring home an animal from abroad." This campaign was highly effective in educating the public and successfully helped keep Ireland rabies-free.

The "Worrying Sheep" Advertising Campaign

A serious issue for Irish farmers in the 1980s was dogs worrying sheep. TV campaigns, often from organizations like the Irish Farmers' Association or FBD insurance, used dramatic ads showing serene fields disrupted by unleashed dogs. The central message was a direct warning to dog owners: "Keep your dog on a leash" and "Your dog, your responsibility," highlighting the legal and moral duty to protect livestock.

Belleek China:

Belleek China prominently features the Irish Wolfhound as a recurring and meaningful motif. The pottery's backstamp, which serves as a key company trademark, consistently includes the wolfhound alongside other iconic Irish symbols such as the round tower—believed to be modeled on the Devenish Round Tower in County Fermanagh—and the Irish harp. This emblematic combination has been part of Belleek's identity since its founding in 1857, symbolizing Irish heritage and craftsmanship. Over the decades, Belleek has employed various versions of this trademark in different colors like black, green, blue, and brown, adapting slightly for special occasions such as the Millennium and anniversary celebrations while retaining the core motifs. The Irish wolfhound's presence in this mark underscores its national significance and iconic status. In addition to the trademark, Belleek has produced limited-edition figurines and collector pieces dedicated specifically to the Irish Wolfhound, celebrating the breed's deep connection to Irish culture and Belleek's artistic tradition. These pieces are highly prized among collectors worldwide, representing not only fine porcelain art but also a proud Irish legacy.

Conclusion

Dogs have woven themselves into the fabric of Irish culture, from the mythical hounds of ancient legends to the internet-famous dogs of today. This journey through literature, film, music, and daily life has shown that dogs in Ireland are far more than just pets, they are an integral part of the nation's cultural identity. They have served as noble symbols on currency and in advertisements, as sources of humor and satire in our greatest works of literature, and as features in heartwarming tales of loss and reunion.

Consider the powerful imagery of the Irish Wolfhound, a breed so central to Celtic mythology that it became a symbol of national pride and strength. In sagas like the Táin Bó Cúailnge, the hero Cú Chulainn (meaning "Hound of Culann") earns his name through an act of loyalty and bravery, embodying the very ideals of the Irish warrior. This legacy continues today, with the Wolfhound appearing in everything from historical art to modern-day advertising campaigns, representing the country's unyielding spirit.

Beyond mythology, dogs are a constant, comforting presence in everyday life. The sight of a mischievous terrier in a rural pub or a beloved golden retriever on Dublin city street is a common one. These animals are celebrated for their personalities, often becoming local celebrities. This deep affection is reflected in our storytelling, where dogs are not just supporting characters but central figures whose loyalty, humor, and resilience mirror our own.

Whether a dog is a mischievous scamp stealing dinner or a viral star making us laugh with a funny song, they reflect the very best of us. They are a constant presence in our pubs and homes, on our mountainsides and beaches—a reflection of a bond that is both ancient and timeless.

-About the Author-
-Séamus Mullarkey...

I love animals and Ireland in equal measure.

— If you love Ireland, you'll love my books —

So, why not join my fan club? You can read all my new books FOR FREE!

AND... You'll get a free excerpt from…,

"Strange and Surprising Ireland" ...

https://www.mullarkeysbooks.org/interestingireland

Please leave a review...

If this book brought you a few moments of pleasure, I'd be so grateful if you took just a few moments to leave a review on the book's Amazon page.

You can get to the review page with the QR code below. Thanks!

Please!

"le do thoil" (leh duh hull)

Recommended Further Reading

One of the great pleasures in writing this book was being able to read so many other fascinating books and articles on dogs and the role they played in Irish culture, both as research and as inspiration. If you'd like a learned and all-encompassing dive into all aspects of Irish dog culture, including a comprehensive background on breeders and breed clubs down through the centuries, David Blake Knox's scholarly and entertaining book, *The Curious History of Irish Dogs* is a pleasure and an education. It's readily available online and in bookstores. If you can source a copy of Anna Redlich's *The Dogs of Ireland*, published in 1949 and reprinted in 1981, please snap it up. It's out of print but makes a great addition to any serious dog lover's library. Online, https://www.duchas.ie/en, is your gateway to everything related to Irish folklore and heritage. With written, photographic, and audio sections, you could probably spend months researching and enjoying just about every aspect of Irish culture. It's available in English and, as Gaeilge (in Irish).

If you're interested in reading more of my books on Irish culture, I'd recommend *Strange and Surprising Ireland: The People, The Land, The Odd, and the Extraordinary* for a broad sweep through the more unusual aspects of Irish history. You might also enjoy *Feck You I'm Irish*, written under the pen name Rashers Tierney, a feisty and irreverent look at why the Irish are so amazing. For those enamored of Ireland's symbol of love, I've written *The History of the Claddagh Ring*. And, for the cat lovers out there, you must check out *The Cats of Ireland* and *101 Ways to Know if Your Cat is Irish*. Finally, if you're planning a trip to Ireland and are looking for an illustrated keepsake journal, look for *The Ireland Travel Journal*, from Mullarkey's Books of Ireland, in which you can record your Irish trip as a treasured reminder of all the fun you've had!

More From Seamus Mullarkey

Would you like to read more of my books???

Just scan below…

STRANGE AND SURPRISING IRELAND:

THE LAND, THE PEOPLE, THE ODD, THE EXTRORDINARY

More From Seamus Mullarkey

Would you like to read more of my books???

Just scan below…

THE HISTORY OF THE CLADDAGH RING

More From Seamus Mullarkey

Would you like to read more of my books???

Just scan below...

F*CK YOU I'M IRISH: WHY WE IRISH ARE SO AWESOME

More From Seamus Mullarkey

Would you like to read more of my books???

Just click or scan below…

More From Seamus Mullarkey

Would you like to read more of my books???

Just scan below…

101 WAYS TO KNOW IF YOUR CAT IS IRISH

More From Seamus Mullarkey

Would you like to read more of my books???

Just scan below…

IRELAND TRAVEL JOURNAL:

AN ILLUSTRATED DIARY AND KEEPSAKE OF YOUR TRIP TO IRELAND

DON'T MISS THIS SPECIAL BONUS

Do you want to learn more about Ireland?

This BONUS book has fascinating trivia, interesting tales and compelling stories about Ireland that you won't find elsewhere…

DOWNLOAD YOUR COPY FOR FREE

https://www.mullarkeysbooks.org/interestingireland

Follow Me

...THERE'S LOTS MORE TO COME...

Scan the code so you

get notified the minute I release a new book...

SCAN TO FOLLOW ME...

Disclaimer

This book is for entertainment purposes only. Under no circumstances will any legal responsibility or blame be held against the publisher for any reparation, damages, or monetary loss due to the text or images herein, either directly or indirectly. Every effort has been made to ensure the historical accuracy of the information contained herein. However, due to the incompleteness and sometimes contradictory nature of historical sources, no attestations are made to claim complete historical accuracy.

www.ingramcontent.com/pod-product-compliance
Lightning Source LLC
LaVergne TN
LVHW011425080426
835512LV00005B/270